PRAISE FOR
LEADING WITH THE HEART

"You can mix unlimited academic expectations with unlimited winning. That's what Coach K has proven at Duke.... Isn't Duke where you would want your son to play?"
— *USA Today*

"His breezy approach is direct and simple: What's most important is working as a team toward a common goal — not necessarily to win the game, but to play the best possible game."
— *Publishers Weekly*

"Unlike other coaches turned business gurus, Coach K doesn't overemphasize the connection between coaching strategy and workplace success. Mostly he talks about the basketball program at Duke and how he fosters the teamwork that is a Blue Devil trademark."
— *Booklist*

"Coach K conducts a clinic on team-building, earning trust, dealing with adversity, and bringing out the best in people."
— *Syracuse Herald-American*

"An excellent book on coaching and leadership principles."
— *Library Journal*

"An extraordinary celebration of human potential, family ties, and personal excellence that not only reveals the philosophy behind his own personal success but the reasons why it can work for anyone."
— *Business Life Magazine*

LEADING
WITH THE
HEART

COACH K'S
Successful Strategies for
Basketball, Business, and Life

MIKE KRZYZEWSKI
WITH DONALD T. PHILLIPS

GRAND
CENTRAL

NEW YORK   BOSTON

Grand Central Publishing
Hachette Book Group
1290 Avenue of the Americas, New York, NY 10104
grandcentralpublishing.com
twitter.com/grandcentralpub

Originally published in hardcover by Warner Books, Inc. in March 2000
First trade paperback edition: March 2001
Reissued by Grand Central Publishing: March 2023

Grand Central Publishing is a division of Hachette Book Group, Inc.
The Grand Central Publishing name and logo is a trademark of Hachette Book Group, Inc.

The publisher is not responsible for websites (or their content) that are not owned by the publisher.

The Hachette Speakers Bureau provides a wide range of authors for speaking events. To find out more, go to hachettespeakersbureau.com or email HachetteSpeakers@hbgusa.com.

Grand Central Publishing books may be purchased in bulk for business, educational, or promotional use. For information, please contact your local bookseller or the Hachette Book Group Special Markets Department at special.markets@hbgusa.com.

Print book interior design by H. Roberts Design.

Library of Congress Cataloging-in-Publication Data

Krzyzewski, Mike
    Leading with the heart : Coach K's successful strategies for basketball, business, and life / Mike Krzyzewski with Donald T. Phillips.
        p.   cm.
    Includes index.
    ISBN 0-446-52626-6
    1. Success.   2. Sports—Psychological aspects.   3. Coaches (Athletics)—Conduct of life.   I. Phillips, Donald T. (Donald Thomas). 1952–   II. Title.

GV706.55 .K79 2000
796.323'63—dc21
                                                                            99-048672

ISBN: 9781538741610 (trade paperback)

Printed in the United States of America

LSC-C

Printing 4, 2023

Dedicated to my brother, Bill,
who has the biggest heart of all

CONTENTS

FOREWORD

*D*uring high school, I was heavily recruited to play basketball at a variety of colleges and universities. Many coaches assured me that I would start or that I would get a certain amount of playing time. Some promised me the world. But not Mike Krzyzewski of Duke University.

"I'm not going to promise you anything," Coach K told me. "If you choose Duke, you have to come in, work hard, and earn everything you receive."

That really stuck with me. It also impressed my parents. And we began to believe that, by playing for him, I might not only become a better ballplayer, but a better person.

Then I visited Duke for the first time and attended the annual basketball awards banquet held at the conclusion of each season. The atmosphere was joyous and friendly, almost like a family reunion. I was most impressed with a speech made by departing senior Quin Snyder, who listed certain values he had learned from Coach K. They included: commitment, toughness, honesty, integrity, collective responsibility, pride, love, and friendship. Both Quin and people in the audience were choking back tears. After hearing that speech, there was never any doubt that I'd go to Duke.

My first team meeting in the fall of 1990 was an awesome day. I remember being excited, anxious, and nervous when Coach K walked in. He paused for a moment to make sure that we were all looking him straight in the eye. And the first thing he said was: "We're going to win the national championship this year."

I later learned that he had never before said that at an opening meeting—and he would rarely ever say it again. It was a remarkable statement for him to make because he had lost three starters from the previous year's team. And *that* team had suffered an embarrassing 30-point loss to UNLV in the national championship game. "Is this man crazy?" I remember wondering. But when the meeting was over, I walked out of the locker room believing we were, indeed, going to win the national championship. That's one of Coach K's most valuable qualities. He's inspiring. He makes you a believer.

We did win the national championship that year, the first in Duke's history. And we won it the next year, too. As a matter of fact, in my four years playing for him, I participated in three Final Fours and three national championship games. More important, however, were the lessons I learned from Coach K about life and leadership. They include: setting the bar high so that you can strive to be the best you can be; the value and rewards of a hard-work ethic; building close relationships based on trust; setting shared goals; sacrificing; giving of yourself; winning with humility; losing with dignity;

turning a negative into a positive; being a part of something bigger than yourself; enjoying the journey.

By attending Duke University, I joined more than a basketball team. I became part of a legacy. In a coaching career that spans more than a quarter century, Coach K's achievements are extraordinary. Fifteen NCAA tournament bids and the highest winning percentage in NCAA tournament history. Eight Final Fours in fourteen years. The only back-to-back national championships in the last twenty-five years. Six years as national Coach of the Year. Five-time ACC Coach of the Year. A career winning percentage of .717. An impeccable reputation for honesty and integrity that is unquestioned in the sports world. And thousands of friends.

Coach K has shown he can win with a lot of talent—and he's shown he can win with a little bit of talent. He brings kids in from all around the country, from different cultures and different backgrounds. He teaches them to transcend their differences for a greater good. He helps them learn to get along together, to work as a team, to respect one another, to care for one another.

I know. I was one of those kids.

They say that "patience and the mulberry leaf in time form a silk gown." As a freshman, I had doubts about myself. I thought I wasn't good enough to play at Duke, that I was in over my head. But Coach K always felt I was better than I ever believed I could be. He constantly reassured me. He told me that I would be something special. It took a while for me to believe in myself. But he always believed in me. And he was patient. With time, he helped me develop my skills as a player and he helped me gain the confidence I needed to make it to the NBA.

But the most important thing of all about Coach K is that

he taught me principles and values that I will carry with me for the rest of my life. Those principles and values transcend basketball. They can be a guide for success in whatever you do in life—whether it's running a big business, ministering to a church, coaching a sports team, or simply trying to achieve your dreams.

When I was very young, my father used to tell me that an army of deer led by a lion will defeat an army of lions led by a deer. At Duke, Coach K was our lion. He was also our friend, our mentor, our coach, our leader.

I graduated years ago, but I'm closer with Coach K now than I was in college—and we were very close back then. Today, I'm proud to say we're good friends. And I know that's the case with a lot of his former players.

When I look back on my time at Duke, I feel lucky to have played for him. I took it for granted then. I was young. I didn't realize what I had. But I appreciate it now. In fact, I appreciate it more and more as the years slip by.

I wish I could go back and relive that experience. I wish I could be a freshman at that first meeting in the team locker room. I wish I could look into Coach K's eyes and hear him tell me, once again, that I was something special.

—Grant Hill
July 1999

PRESEASON

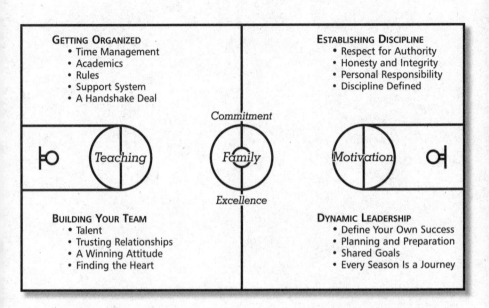

GETTING ORGANIZED
- Time Management
- Academics
- Rules
- Support System
- A Handshake Deal

ESTABLISHING DISCIPLINE
- Respect for Authority
- Honesty and Integrity
- Personal Responsibility
- Discipline Defined

Commitment

Teaching   *Family*   *Motivation*

Excellence

BUILDING YOUR TEAM
- Talent
- Trusting Relationships
- A Winning Attitude
- Finding the Heart

DYNAMIC LEADERSHIP
- Define Your Own Success
- Planning and Preparation
- Shared Goals
- Every Season Is a Journey

"My goal in preseason is to get to know my players and what they can do. My total focus is finding out who we are and developing a personality on our team."

—COACH K

1

GETTING
ORGANIZED

"Too many rules get in the way of leadership. They just put you in a box. . . . People set rules to keep from making decisions."

—**Coach K**

"The deal is the handshake. The deal is that there won't be any deals."

—**Coach K**

"Every team I was on over my four years at Duke, he coached differently."

—**Grant Hill (1990–1994) on Coach K**

*O*kay, everybody, listen up.

"We have only one rule here: Don't do anything that's detrimental to yourself. Because if it's detrimental to you, it'll be detrimental to our program and to Duke University."

As the team gathers together in our locker room for the first time, I try to get my only rule out of the way fast. I won't dwell on it because I'd rather not ruin the moment. *This* is a great day—a day that I've been looking forward to with anxious anticipation for months. You can *feel* the excitement in the air. You can *see* the spring in everyone's step.

Even though the preseason begins around the first of September, it's really like springtime—time for the birth of a new team. All the players come in fresh. They bring whoever they are to that first meeting. They bring innocence with them. And they're ready to grow.

Looking at the young faces in front of me, I see myself more than thirty years earlier. And I think back to 1969.

"I want to tell you a story," I'll say next. "It's a story about how I first became a basketball coach.

"In 1969, right after I graduated from West Point, I was assigned to Fort Carson, Colorado. One of the first things I did was begin to work out and play in my off-duty hours with the post basketball team. But my direct superior, a colonel, called me in and told me that I could not participate. He didn't like the thought of me fraternizing with the enlisted men.

" 'No officer of mine is going to be wasting his time playing basketball,' he said. 'There are other things you should be doing.'

"Shortly after that, I received a call from Major General Bernard Rogers, the new division commander at Fort Carson. General Rogers had just received that assignment after having served as the commandant of cadets at West Point, where, of course, he knew me as the captain of the varsity basketball team. The general had just been to a post basketball game and he called to ask why I wasn't playing with the team.

" 'Sir, my colonel would rather that I not play,' I responded. 'He feels it's not a good thing for officers to do.'

"The general then went to the colonel.

" 'Why isn't Lieutenant Krzyzewski playing on the post basketball team?' he asked.

"When the colonel responded that he just didn't think it was good for an officer to participate, General Rogers replied: 'Well, Colonel, the question is not, "Should Lieutenant Krzyzewski be playing basketball on our team." The question is, "Should we *have* a team?" If the answer to that question is, "Yes, we should have a team," then we should have *the best damn team we can possibly have.*'

5

"The colonel then agreed that the post should have a basketball team.

" 'Well, Colonel,' said the general, 'then Lieutenant Krzyzewski *will* play basketball. And not only that, he will *coach* the team.'

"That's how I began coaching basketball. And the first year, we won the Fifth Army championship. General Rogers eventually became the Army Chief of Staff and the Supreme Allied Commander in Europe.

"But that's not why I'm telling you this story," I'll say in conclusion. "There's already been a decision made here at Duke that we're going to have a basketball team. So *we're going to have the best damn team we can possibly have.* That's why all of you are here today. You were recruited specifically for this purpose. Each of you is special. I don't want you to ever forget that."

Even though our first formal practice is still six weeks away, I'm already comfortable with the kids on the team. I've spent a good deal of time recruiting them from all over the country. At Duke, we search for good kids with strong character—not necessarily kids with great talent who can play, but great individuals who are willing to be part of a team and who are coachable. Some of the students have been with us for one, two, or three years—and some are incoming freshmen. I've worked hard to get to know all of them. And even if I don't yet understand every aspect of their personalities, at least I know the fabric of who they are. I like them as players and as people.

We usually have the initial meeting in our locker room because it's where we're going to be for many intimate moments in the future. So I think it's a good place for us to take that first step. In addition to the players, the rest of the team is present, including: the trainer, the team physician, the managers, my administrative assistant, and our three assistant coaches.

It's important to begin using plural pronouns right away. "Our" instead of "my." "We" instead of "I." "Us" rather than "me." I don't want the guys to be thinking this is "my" team— Coach K's team. I want them to believe it's "our" team.

The principle that "we're all important" is also something that needs to be demonstrated immediately. That's why the head coach isn't the only one who talks at this, or any other, Duke basketball meeting. Different people will speak to the players. The team trainer will discuss schedules for upcoming physicals. The team managers will say something about what they do and what is expected. Then I'll usually pop in with something like: "Just remember, the managers are part of our team—as is everyone here. Treat them right. We're all equal."

Time Management

At the first meeting, we pass out notebooks and pocket calendars containing a variety of logistical items. Important dates for the upcoming semester are marked and reviewed, including things like: our first practice, the day new recruits are in town for a visit, special events at my home, and, of course, our schedule of games.

We'll also point out when fall break occurs, and when might be a good time to leave for the Christmas holidays. We'll encourage the students to plan ahead, to schedule their flights and trips well in advance so as to save money.

Time management is a lesson that the students learn through us—not only as it relates to them individually, but as it pertains to a group. In other words, we make certain that they realize right off the bat that they have responsibilities to the team as well as to themselves alone.

Academics

We also really hit hard on academics. One member of our staff will talk about the students getting their schedules set up and in on time. They will be reminded to tell professors of their athletic schedules, when they have to miss class, and what they plan to do to get the materials they would miss.

Basketball players are simply not going to scrape by in their studies at Duke University. They are going to have to work. As a head coach, I personally do not want to represent a school that brings in twenty people over five years and have only two of them graduate. I expect every player we recruit to graduate. And I tell them so right up front.

We also want university life to be a total experience for them. That's one reason there are no athletic dorms on campus. They just serve to separate the athlete from the rest of the student body and rob him of the opportunity to integrate with others. To me, that's one of the most important aspects of a college education.

While it's always up to the individual student to graduate, I also believe it's incumbent upon the school to positively influence its athletes in their studies. So, throughout the year, we keep close track of how our players are progressing. Once the schedules are in, we obtain a syllabus for each course so that we know when project due dates and midterm tests will occur. As the head coach, I receive weekly updates throughout the year on significant events in each student's academic life—and then take action accordingly.

At the first team meeting, I'll take a minute to stress honor in academics. "What is the worst thing that can happen to you academically?" I'll ask. And usually someone will respond by saying, "I get an F."

"No, that's not the worst thing," will be my comeback. "You can get an F even though you may try like crazy. The worst thing you can do is cheat. Now what do we mean by cheating? Well it's easy to copy off of someone else's paper, use someone else's paper, bring information into a test that you're not allowed to bring in, things like that. But let me tell you that here in the Duke basketball program, all those things are absolutely unacceptable."

And then I'll explore the issue somewhat deeper.

"Now, *why* would you cheat? *Why* would you cut corners? Well, time puts more pressure on you than anything else. That's one reason we're trying to teach you effective time management. In other words, if we know when your paper is due, we can remind you so you're not waiting until the last minute.

"Fellas, don't put yourself in a position where you have to cheat. That's the worst thing you can do as a Duke basketball player. If it happens, you're going to be punished severely by the school—and I'll support that punishment, whatever it is. But we should never get to that point. If you just say to me, 'I'm stuck or I'm in trouble,' then we'll work on it together. We'll be there to help you. But you also have to learn to help yourself."

Rules

At our first meeting, I give the team only one rule to live by. And it's pretty general, at that, because "not doing anything detrimental to yourself" covers a lot of things. It includes drinking at two o'clock in the morning, taking drugs, cheating in academics, and so on. Of course, the only one mentioned specifically is "no cheating." But I don't have to tell the players all the details. The upperclassmen will spend time letting the freshmen know what is expected. That, in turn, fosters additional leadership. And leadership on any team should be plural, not singular.

Too many rules get in the way of leadership. They just put you in a box and, sooner or later, a rule-happy leader will wind up in a situation where he wants to use some discretion but is forced to go along with some decree that he himself has concocted.

Of course, a few leaders like to be backed up by a long list of do's and don'ts. "OOPS, you did this on the list. I got'cha." Well, I don't want to be a team of "I got'chas." I got'cha means "I" rather than "we." And a leader who sets too many rules is making it appear that it is "my" team, rather than "our" team.

The truth is that many people set rules to keep from making decisions. Not me. I don't want to be a manager or a dictator. I want to be a leader—and leadership is ongoing, adjustable, flexible, and dynamic. As such, leaders have to maintain a certain amount of discretion.

At times, there may be extenuating circumstances for a person violating a rule. Take being late for practice as an example. If a senior like Tommy Amaker, who's done everything right for nearly four years, is suddenly late for a team bus or a team meeting, I would wait a couple of minutes for him. He's built up trust by being on time over the long haul. Well, when he finally shows up, Tommy will look me in the eye and tell me why he was late. He might say, "Coach, my car broke down and

I don't have a car phone. I ran all the way here." Or he might say, "Coach, I just screwed up. No excuse."

However, with a new player who has yet to build trust, I might be less flexible. I recall, for instance, when freshmen Johnny Dawkins and Mark Alarie were late for a team bus. We didn't know where they were, they had not called, and every other member of the team was on time. So we left them behind. Eventually, the two caught up to us and I remember being ready to hammer them. But after hearing that they had overslept, I began to wonder why other members of our team had not checked up on them. So I talked to the entire team about setting up a buddy system where everyone looked out for one another. "If one of us is late," I told them, "all of us are late." Now if I had punished Mark and Johnny and let that end the matter, I would never have gotten to the heart of the problem.

The fact that I *don't* have a hard and fast rule gives me flexibility in cases like these. It provides me the latitude to lead. It also allows me to show that I care about the kids on my team and it demonstrates that I'm trying to be fair-minded.

When Johnny and Mark explained their situation to me, they looked me straight in the eye—and I could tell they were being truthful and sincere. Throughout the season, I look into my players' eyes to gauge feelings, confidence levels, and to establish instant trust. Most of the time, they won't quibble with me—and they certainly can't hide their feelings from what their eyes reveal. So I ask all members of our team to look each other in the eye when speaking to one another. It's a principle we live by.

I know that when my wife, Mickie, and I look at each other, we know what we're going to say is the truth. And we've tried to teach our daughters, Debbie, Lindy, and Jamie, the same thing. "Look each other straight in the eye, tell the truth, full disclosure." And as our daughters have gotten older, they've really become our friends. They knew that their mom and I weren't going to chew their heads off every time they talked to us. Rather, we were going to be there for them.

Support System

It was exactly this type of family environment in which I was raised—in a Polish neighborhood in Chicago where there were always flowers outside the homes, where people swept the sidewalks and the streets themselves. Whatever you had, you took care of. And, usually, the kids had more than the parents. In our neighborhood, there was total commitment to the development of the children.

My brother, Bill, and I were particularly lucky. Our dad, William, was an elevator operator in Willoughby Tower in downtown Chicago. Our mom, Emily, was a homemaker and a cleaning woman who scrubbed floors at the Chicago Athletic Club. I saw little of my dad because he worked nearly all the time and we didn't talk much. That's the way ethnic families were back then. But my mom was always, always there for me.

My parents had little in the way of material things. In fact, I remember that in my mom's closet there were always two dresses. They were clean and they were in great shape. But there were only two. My parents were people who never had anything, but they had everything. There was a lot of love and a lot of pride in our house.

It was easy for me growing up because I was always surrounded by a support system. And as I got older, I wondered what gave my mother, my father, my brother, and my best friend, Moe Mlynski, the ability to feel good about what I did. The fact is that whatever happened to me happened to them, too.

The best example I can think of involves sports. I was fairly successful as a point guard in basketball when I attended Weber High School, an all-boys Catholic prep school, which, by the way, my parents paid extra money to send me to. Moe went to Gordon Tech, which was our rival. But when we'd play Gordon, Moe was always cheering for *me*. And when I had a good game, he'd come up to me and say, "Hey, Mick (my nickname back then), that was a great game." And I could see in his eyes that he was really happy, that he really meant it.

Then Moe would drive me home. Actually, he was the only guy in our group who had a car. And during the entire ride home, he'd tell me how great I was during the game. And when I got to the house, my mom would be waiting up—not to check on me, but to talk to me a little bit. She may have even been at the game. Sometimes she'd go and not tell me and I wouldn't even realize she was in the stands.

Mom would tell me that I played a great game. "I'm very proud of you," she'd say over and over again. And then she'd ask me how I felt. Somehow, just the fact that she would wait up, that she would take the time, meant more to me than the actual conversation.

Anything that I felt good about, my mom and dad felt better about. Everything that I did was supported. I think this type of sustenance had a lot to do with me being confident as an adult. For some reason, I'm not afraid to lose. I wasn't back then, and I'm not now.

In general, I'd like to think that what my mom felt about me, I can feel about the players on our Duke basketball team. If I can provide that kind of support system for our team—

where the managers feel good, the assistants feel good, the freshman feels good about the senior, and the senior about the sophomore, and so on—then we're going to be that much stronger a team.

Not only that—it's a pure kind of feeling. That kind of support system—the family kind of support system—is like getting a shot to keep away jealousy. Your culture doesn't allow jealousy. That's what the best families are all about. There's real love, real caring, pride in one another's accomplishments, and no jealousy.

So we emphasize at our initial team meeting that the new guys are not just joining a basketball team, but a basketball family. We then hand out laminated cards that include the home and business phone numbers of every member of the team—including players, assistant coaches, and so on.

"Carry this card around," we tell them. "And whenever you're in harm's way, make a call. If it's two o'clock in the morning and you're in trouble, someone on this card will help you. When there's a chance to make a mistake, remember that you're part of our family. Remember that you're not alone. And remember that whatever happens to you, happens to all of us."

As a coach, as a leader, I'm going to provide that safety net—that family support system. And all I'm really doing is passing along something that was given to me many years ago.

A Handshake Deal

Long before the first team meeting, during the recruiting process, I've made a handshake deal with every one of our players.

To each kid, I say: "I'm going to give you my best. I'm going to give you 100 percent. In return, I expect you to graduate. You'll be coming to Duke for more than just basketball. If you don't understand that, then don't come to Duke. I want you to be passionate about basketball, but I also want you to obtain a great education."

That early conversation usually works out very well. But every now and then, a new recruit will ask me to promise that he'll be a starter or that he'll get a certain amount of playing time each game. I won't do that. I'll promise him only that I'll be honest and fair—and that he'll be rewarded on his performance.

This is my "fair but not equal" policy. I'll be "fair" in everything I do, but the players won't be "equal" with regard to on-the-court playing time. If I gave everybody equal playing time, it wouldn't be fair to the team as a whole. That's because the group may be more effective if Johnny Dawkins plays thirty minutes and Tommy Amaker plays ten. It also wouldn't be fair to individual members of the team. If, through hard work and excellent performance, Dawkins demonstrates he deserves thirty minutes of playing time, he should get thirty minutes of playing time. People who deserve to do more should do more.

This handshake agreement is a clean and honest deal. There are no hidden agendas. Everything straight up front and nothing behind anybody's back. Every kid can look around the room and know that I didn't promise anyone that they'd be a starter. The deal is the handshake. The deal is that there won't be any deals.

Mutual commitment helps overcome the fear of failure—especially when people are part of a team sharing and achieving goals. It also sets the stage for open dialogue and honest conversation. Early in the preseason, I'll often have a casual conversation with one of our players about his personal life. And because we already have that commitment to each other, it's easy for us to talk. He already knows that I'm on his side and that I'll always be there for him.

The same principle holds in business when, for example, a manager walks in and talks to an employee about something other than a job assignment. It shows not only that the leader cares, but that he also might know a little something about the employee's personal life. In general, it's another way of helping people feel like they're part of the unit. I think it's very important for leaders to take time throughout the year to show they care. Ongoing communication reinforces the handshake.

I'm always really excited at the beginning of each first team meeting. But the exhilaration I feel being with the team causes me to be even more excited toward the end of the meeting. That's because for nearly an hour—and for the first time—I've been interacting with them as a group rather than only as individuals.

But every meeting has to end, so I usually wrap up this one by first giving the guys some advice about the coming year. For instance, I may ask them to concentrate on individual physical conditioning over the coming six weeks so that they are in really good shape by mid-October's first day of practice. And almost always, I will remind them about their studies. "It's September, fellas, and you should think about getting off to a good start academically," I'll say. "Once practice begins, things will get busy in a hurry. Remember that you'll be a better player if you're not behind in your studies."

Grant Hill once perceptively remarked that every team he played on during his four years at Duke, I coached differently. Actually, every team I've had in my coaching career, I've coached differently. That's because each year brings with it a new team, with new people who have different personalities and different skills. If I hope to get the most out of these players as a group, I *have* to coach them differently than previous teams.

I believe that each team has to run its own race. So when I conclude our first meeting by providing a glimpse of where I think we're headed, part of what I say will depend largely on the guys sitting in the locker room. I might tell them that we're going to have a lot of fun this year, that we're going to grow as a team. Or I could tell them that we have a chance to be a really good team. Heck, I may even say that I think we can win the national championship. But whatever I tell them will be realistic and something that I believe in my heart.

By this time, I'm really anxious to get started. Not knowing how the season is going to go is stimulating for me. And the anticipation of the upcoming journey is so exciting that I get goose bumps on my arms and legs—something the players often notice. Jay Bilas, for instance, once told me that he could never remember questioning me or my commitment to the things I was saying to him and the other players. "When Coach K got those goose bumps, you knew he was not giving you some 'rah-rah' speech," said Bilas. "You can't fake goose bumps."

After gaining everyone's complete attention—so that they're all looking me straight in the eye—I will say one final thing to them. I'll say:

"I'm really looking forward to coaching every one of you this year."

And am I ever.

Coach K's Tips

- Recruit great individuals who are willing to be part of a team and who are coachable.

- It's important to begin using plural pronouns right away: "Our" instead of "my," "we" instead of "I," "us" instead of "me." Remember that leadership on a team is not singular, it's plural.

- Demonstrate the principle "we're all important" by making sure that you are not the only one speaking at a meeting.

- Teach time management, not only as it relates to individuals, but as it pertains to a group.

- Stress honor in all things.

- Don't be a team of "I got'chas." Too many rules get in the way of leadership.

- Preserve the latitude to lead.

- Set up a family support system for your team. It's like getting a shot to keep away jealousy.

- Hand out a laminated card with the telephone numbers of the players and staff. Remind them to call somebody when they're in harm's way.

- Believe in a handshake.

- Mutual commitment helps people overcome the fear of failure.

- Each team has to run its own race.

2

BUILDING YOUR TEAM

"When you first assemble a group, it's not a team right off the bat. It's only a collection of individuals."

—Coach K

"Leaders have to search for the heart on a team, because the person who has it can bring out the best in everybody else."

—Coach K

"Sometimes a loss can be a win."

—Coach K

I've been forming teams since I was a kid in Chicago. It's what I enjoy most in life. It's what I do.

During the Chicago summers, when I was about eight or nine years old, all the kids in our neighborhood would leave our houses in the morning and might not come back until it got dark. Maybe we'd go home for a quick lunch, but that was it.

"Mike, where are you going?" my mom would ask as I headed out the door.

"I'm going to the schoolyard to play."

"Okay," she'd say.

I didn't have to tell her who I was playing with or what time I'd be home. She already knew. Life was good back then. It was innocent.

My buddies were Moe, Porky, Twams, Sell, and about a dozen other guys. We called ourselves "The Columbos," after the Columbus grade school where we played. We weren't a gang as some people think of it today. We were just a bunch of boys who got together every day at the corner of Augusta Boulevard and Leavitt Avenue. The school was a city block away from my house and it was safe. One area of the yard was paved; another part was crushed stone. There was a basketball hoop on one end, and on the other an area large enough to play baseball.

We had no organized sports in our community back in the mid-1950s. It just wasn't a big thing. *We* were the coaches. *We* were the players. If eight kids showed up, we played four-on-four baseball. If only two of us came out, then we drew a box on the wall of the schoolyard and played fast pitch with a rubber ball. But most of the time, we had between eight and twelve kids show up on any given day. I was usually the guy who split the teams. I just took the initiative to get something going. Instead of standing around, I'd say, "Okay, we're going to play five-on-five. Let's go."

I remember the time I pulled together a group of guys from my school, St. Helen's, and formed a basketball team. This was my first stab at formal coaching. I was twelve years old and in the seventh grade.

Our team practiced together regularly and when I thought we were ready, I went to our principal, who was, of course, a nun. I was very direct with her. I said, "Sister, I've organized a basketball team for CYO (Catholic Youth Organization) and I'd like for our school to join so we can play." But because St. Helen's didn't participate in CYO, she said, "No, we're not going to do that."

And I immediately blurted out, "No, you don't understand, we're good."

I think that was the start of my not taking no for an answer.

Our team didn't get into CYO, but that didn't stop us. I called around and set up games with all the other teams. No parents were involved. I just dealt with the kids. "Meet us at Commercial Park, Saturday, two o'clock," I'd say. And everybody would show up.

We played about eight or ten games a season and we won most of them. But there was never a championship game. We were never a part of the league, never in the standings. But we got to play. Back then, it wasn't so much about winning, although we always tried to win. Rather, it was about playing the game for the pure enjoyment of it. In truth, we played for innocence.

Talent

When you first assemble a group, it's not a team right off the bat. It is a collection of individuals, just like any other group. And there is some truth to the adage "You're only as good as your talent." As a matter of fact, I think everyone understands that you can't win championships without talent. So assembling skillful individuals as part of your team is a given. Then, of course, it becomes a matter of motivating those people to perform as a team.

I try to employ really good, smart people who want to be part of my organization. And I try to surround myself with those who are not yes people. I want them to tell me what they really think, good or bad. Usually, I employ six assistants as part of my inner circle—three assistant coaches, a director of basketball operations, a director of academics, and an executive assistant. I really try to hire people I know to be good character-wise—even though they may not have developed all the skills necessary for a particular position.

Actually, I like my three key assistant coaches to be former Duke basketball players. I've already spent four years with them and we have established great relationships. They understand my system. And they know what it is to be a student at Duke. They've lived in the dorms and have had the experience of managing a basketball routine with a full course load. Because they've been in that situation, they'll have great empathy for the current players. And to me, that is a much more important aspect of leadership than having the great technical expertise of someone who's coached for fifteen years elsewhere. Not everyone can know what the players are going through. But everyone, if they're bright, can learn the Xs and Os.

The first of my former players to be hired was Tommy Amaker. That was for the 1988–1989 season and just a few years later we won back-to-back national championships. Tommy had a lot to do with that success. But I found that achievement in our program began to cause greater separation between me, as the head coach, and my players. There were not only more demands on my time, but many of the new kids coming in began viewing me as a top coach in my profession, which just naturally put some distance between us. The passage of time also played a part because the older I became, the less I remembered about my own college experience. In addition, time changes all things and I realized that college life was very different today from when I was a student.

It became clear to me that if I wanted to continue contending for national championships, I was going to have to change some things. So I began searching for ways to complement myself better—which is something every leader should do. Hiring younger assistant coaches, who were closer in age to the current players, seemed like a smart thing to do. And it worked, too. It helped us continue our success of being a serious contender every year.

Maintaining a successful program can be much more difficult than building one. When a small business starts out, for example, there is always a lot of personal interaction among the core team. As a result, success can build rapidly. But what happens when that little company starts to expand with offices in six different cities? The close, tight-knit camaraderie that originally fostered success is much more difficult to achieve and sustain. Well, if I'm the leader of the company, I would want someone running the satellite offices with whom I already have a close relationship. I'd hire people like Amaker, Bob Bender, Pete Gaudet, Chuck Swenson, Mike Dement, Tim O'Toole, Mike Brey, Jay Bilas, Quin Snyder, Johnny Dawkins, David Henderson, and Steve Wojciechowski—all of whom have worked with me as assistant coaches.

Many of these guys have gone on to become head coaches themselves. And, actually, I prefer that all our assistant coaches have the vision of being head coaches. That way, they'll want to learn and grow.

Of course, it also creates a situation where, every couple of years or so, we'll have a vacancy on the coaching staff. Then we're forced to hire a new person to fill the void. But the last thing in the world I want to do is force a new employee into a preexisting job description. As a matter of fact, I really dislike job descriptions. They tend to put people in boxes and hold them back from realizing their full potential. Rather, I prefer to reevaluate our entire team and match the needs of the program with the strengths of the individuals running the program. I never let a person's weakness get in the way of his strength.

In 1999, for instance, Quin Snyder was named head basketball coach at the University of Missouri. After we hired Steve Wojciechowski to fill the void, I sat down with my entire staff and looked at the coming year to determine what we needed to get done. Then we assigned individuals to tasks according to their skills, abilities, and personal interests. Johnny Dawkins became my lead assistant—but his responsibilities were not exactly the same as those of Quin Snyder, who was my lead assistant the previous year. Whereas Quin was primarily responsible for recruiting, we all felt it was better for Johnny not to go on the road because of his exceptional skill with individual player development. So Wojo was given principal responsibility for recruiting—which fit him to a tee. And we set other job assignments similarly.

In reality, our assistants know that I might change things around *every* year—even if we don't have any personnel moves. It's basically an appraisal process where I look closely at each individual—what he did well, what he could improve upon, what would be better assigned to another guy, and what he might be able to handle that I might not have previously recognized. Then we make changes accordingly. Moreover, this is an ongoing process throughout the entire year. We adjust as we go—according to needs and circumstances.

Tommy Amaker, also now a head coach, has pointed out that this process gave him a sense of self-importance and confidence—not to mention exposure and experience.

"It not only broadened my horizons and gave me the experience I needed to progress in my career," he said, "it also put me in a position where I had to stretch and grow."

Having young assistants on staff provides an incredible amount of energy and enthusiasm. I also like my former players around because they'll remember things I did years ago— and then remind me so I can employ those things once again if appropriate. And sometimes when I'm in a meeting with them, they remind me of why I'm a coach in the first place. They're my friends, they make me feel good, and they keep me young.

Trusting Relationships

Each team I coach is different because each individual is different. That's the beauty of coaching and it's one of the things I love about each team.

Almost everything in leadership comes back to relationships. And, naturally, the level of cooperation on any team increases tremendously as the level of trust rises. The only way you can possibly lead people is to understand people. And the best way to understand them is to get to know them better.

I like to have a close relationship with every member of our team. And my total focus in the preseason is finding out who we are and developing a personality of our own. So I have the players and coaches over to my house. We go out to eat together. We have impromptu discussions. I goof around with them. In those situations, I see their reactions and I see what I need to do to lead them. They also get to know the kind of person I am.

Leaders have to give time for relationships. But more demands will be placed on their time as they become more successful. So if a person's success is based on developing relationships, then they have to continually find new ways of getting it done. That's one reason I depend on my staff to help me.

I also believe that lasting success involves more than simply building relationships between the leader and other members of the team. Bonds have to form among *all* members of the team—player to player, manager to player, administrative assistant to head coach, head coach to player, head coach to assistant coach, assistant coach to assistant coach, seniors to freshmen, sophomores to juniors, and so on. Every individual must have a trusting relationship with every other member of the team. Now let me explain why.

Visualize a wagon wheel as a complete team. A leader might be the hub of the wheel at the center. Now suppose the spokes are the connecting relationships the leader is building with people on the outer rim of the wheel. If the hub is removed, then the entire wheel collapses. In a situation like that, if a team loses the leader, the entire team collapses.

There was a time in my life when I did have this framework and my wheel did collapse. I've learned this lesson the hard way. A framework of leadership has to be created so that the wheel is sustained if something happens to the hub. You do that by developing trusting relationships among everyone. The team has to go on. The team has to succeed—even if the leader is incapacitated or injured or out for some reason. And when all members have an appreciation for the aspects of every other job on the team, the team survives and continues. In fact, if it's a really close team with strong bonds, they might even have some significant wins as the members rally from adversity.

A Winning Attitude

Whenever I'm building a team, I try to instill a mind-set that the guys are going to win eventually—that our destination is winning. Now that doesn't necessarily mean that the destination is winning the national championship. It means constantly improving to reach maximum potential.

When we play a basketball game, we win it or we lose it. And the outside world defines us based on that win or loss. We're either good or we're bad on that day. Basically that's how most people look at it.

But it's not how I look at it.

When we win a game, everything isn't right. And when we lose a game, everything isn't wrong. As a matter of fact, sometimes a loss can be a win.

If a team played as hard as they possibly could and came up short, did they really lose? I don't think so. I believe that any team that does its best is a winner. If we're constantly looking at a win-loss record to determine whether we are doing well, we're not looking at the right barometer.

A real winning attitude is about standards of excellence— which are variable from year to year, from team to team. Being the best you can be—and doing the best you can—are the constants.

A good example is my talk with Danny Ferry after his junior year when he considered going pro. Danny had made first-team All-America and was Atlantic Coast Conference Player of the Year. Rather than advising him not to jump to the NBA, I simply told him that if he came back to Duke for his senior year, I would expect him to improve.

"If you come back, you have to do better than you did last year," I told him. "You have room to grow and I'm going to demand that you get better. That's the only way I want you back."

Danny did come back and he became a better player. His standard of excellence was raised for that senior year because he had the *potential* to be better.

This concept applies to teams as well as individuals. If you have a better team than you had the previous year, then by definition, it can exceed last year's results. But a better team can and should have a higher standard of excellence.

This is where the leader comes in. The leader has to assess the quality of the team, set the standard of excellence, and then work with the team to achieve that standard—to be the best they can be every time out.

That's what I do. I determine how good our kids can be by watching them, by getting to know them, by building relationships with them. I constantly try to take a realistic look at our team and try not to let the final outcome of any game spike emotions too high or too low. And then I also work with the guys over the course of the entire season to help raise them to their highest potential.

When you view winning the way I do, it becomes clear that leaders are ultimately responsible for how their teams perform—and whether they are the best they can be. But that's not really pressure, it's reality—and it is also a wonderful challenge. I really believe that if a leader is a stickler on high performance, on excellence, then winning games will be a natural by-product.

In building *any* winning team, it's important to remember that the members of the team don't have to be perfect, they just have to keep trying to be the best they can be. That's my definition of a winning attitude.

Finding the Heart

Let me mention three of my past players who were always striving to get better and be the best they could possibly be. Bobby Hurley, Steve Wojciechowski, and Trajan Langdon were all different. But each, in their own way, had tremendous impact whenever they were in the game.

Bobby Hurley came to Duke University from Jersey City and St. Anthony's Catholic high school. He was a point guard.

During the recruiting process, I noticed that there was something special about this kid. He had great daring. When there was a tough situation, instead of backing down, he was constantly moving forward. Literally fearless on the court, he made great plays instinctively. And I love that. I thought I had decent daring when I was in high school. But Bobby Hurley had more daring than I did.

So I told his dad that, for point guard that year, I was going to recruit only Bobby. I really wanted to coach this kid. And for four years, I loved being around him. He gave me back much more than I gave him. And, boy, did he have an inspiring influence on our team during those years—which included two national championships.

Steve Wojciechowski was a point guard from Cardinal Gibbons Catholic high school in Baltimore, Maryland. He was a tremendous emotional leader—and he had passion, great passion. But Wojo didn't start until his junior year. Before that, he played in a reserve role. Part of his development was due to a conversation we had late in his sophomore year. I told him that the way he would be his best in a reserve role was not to accept that role.

"You need to fight to be a starter," I told him.

I also said that he needed to lose some weight. But, in my

mind, I thought that this line of thinking would make him our best backup player. Little did I know, however, that because he ended up fighting so hard, I would have no choice but to make him a starter.

Wojo stormed back from the summer layoff fifteen pounds lighter. And from the first day of practice, it was apparent that his leadership skills had improved dramatically. During preseason practices, I asked members of the team who they'd like to see start. You'd think that many kids might answer, "Me. I'd start me." But every time I asked the guys on the team that question, they would pick Wojciechowski.

That preseason, Wojo fought the more physically talented Trajan Langdon for the key point guard position. And in the process, the two of them became best friends. It actually came to a point where I didn't know who the entire starting team would be, but I knew that Wojo and Trajan were going to be two of the five starters. Langdon because of his exceptional talent, and Wojciechowski because of his heart. And since the other guys on the team recognized how hard these two worked, then I knew everybody would be motivated. And during Wojo's junior year, we ended up winning the league by starting four guards and a six-foot, six-inch forward.

Emotion doesn't necessarily have to be shown with your fists pumping—like Wojo always showed it. Trajan Langdon, a serious kid from Anchorage, Alaska, was incredibly emotional, but in a quiet way.

Like Wojciechowski, he had amazing heart. But his was a different kind of heart—a sturdy heart, an unwavering heart. It was a courage that other people could latch on to. In a stiff wind, it didn't sway. It was there on any and every occasion. If there was a tornado coming, you grabbed ahold of Langdon.

Heart is not easily defined—nor is it obvious to everyone.

31

Hurley's daring is easy to see. So is Wojo's passion. But the quiet heart isn't seen or understood very often. And while the coach has to look for it, it's always known by the players on the court—always.

Just as there are different *elements* of heart, there are different *levels* of heart people possess. For instance, Wojo had daring and Langdon definitely had passion—as do almost all of the players who've played on my teams. In addition, the other members of Hurley's team also had various levels of heart. But all of our hearts would move better when we let Bobby Hurley's heart go—especially mine.

People have to be given the freedom to show the heart they possess. I think it's a leader's responsibility to provide that type of freedom. And I believe it can be done through relationships and family. Because if a team is a real family, its members *want* to show you their hearts.

Leaders have to search for the heart on a team, because the person who has it can bring out the best in everybody else. And if you're fortunate enough to have more than one member with various aspects of heart at high levels, it simply lifts everybody up to that much higher a level of performance—including the leader.

The person with heart inspires the entire team. It's like chemistry. He's the one who makes the formula work—the one element that sets off the explosive reaction.

And I also know this to be true.

When I have a kid like Bobby Hurley on my team, when I'm talking to the group and have eye-to-eye contact with that kid—he makes me a better coach. He motivates me. He makes me better by giving me confidence to do what I feel.

And you know that dark alley you may have to walk through on the way to your destination? I know that I won't have to walk it alone. I know that guy, the guy with the heart, is going with me. I know if I encourage his daring, his passion, or his quiet courage, then he's going to bring out more of the daring and the passion and the courage in *me*—and in every single member of our team.

I'm *always* searching for that in a team. I'm *always* looking to lead with the heart.

Every preseason I ask myself the same question.

Where will the heart be?

COACH K'S TIPS

- All your assistants should have the vision of being a top leader. That way they'll want to learn and grow.

- It's not wise to force a person into a job description. Job descriptions should not be "ready-made." Rather, they should be carved out to fit people on the team.

- Never let a person's weakness get in the way of his strength.

- Go through an appraisal and reevaluation process every year. Rotate some responsibilities.

- The level of cooperation on any team increases tremendously as the level of trust rises.

- Bonds have to form among all members of the team. An architecture of leadership has to be created so that the wheel is sustained if something happens to the hub.

- A real winning attitude is about standards of excellence—which are variable from year to year, from team to team. Being the best you can be—and doing the best you can—are the constants.

- People have to be given the freedom to show the heart they possess.

- Leaders have to search for the heart on a team because the person who has it can bring out the best in everybody else—including the leader.

- Every year, you should ask yourself this question: "Where will the heart be?"

3

ESTABLISHING DISCIPLINE

"If a team cannot perform with excellence at a moment's notice, they probably will fail in the long run."

—Coach K

"Discipline is doing what you are supposed to do in the best possible manner at the time you are supposed to do it. And that's not such a bad thing."

—Coach K

"This isn't all about 'I love you,' and 'Let's hold hands and skip.' It's also about 'Get your rear in gear,' 'What the hell are you doing?' and 'Why aren't you in class?' "

—Coach K

When I was eighteen years old and a senior in high school, Coach Bob Knight, who was the head basketball coach at West Point, offered to get me an appointment to the United States Military Academy. I knew it was a great honor and I was really excited about playing basketball for him at the college level.

But I didn't want to go. I didn't want to be a soldier. I wanted to be a teacher and a coach. So I told my parents that I was going to turn down Knight's offer and go somewhere else.

Well, my mom and dad didn't like that decision. So one day, they staged a conversation in the kitchen while I was working in the living room. I say "staged" because, as I look back on it, I'm certain they planned it out well in advance.

They were speaking mostly in Polish with animated tones.

I didn't understand Polish, but it was clear I was getting hammered.

First of all, I knew it was important because whenever they didn't want me to hear something important, they spoke in Polish. Second, I got a few hints by some things they threw into the conversation, things like: "West Point" and "Mike . . . stupid!"

My parents knew me better than I knew myself. And as I grew older, I appreciated their approach to the situation. They didn't simply say to themselves, "Gosh, I don't want my son coming back to me saying that I forced him into it." Rather, they took the view that they knew what was best for their kid and they were going to tell me so.

The kitchen discussion was their way of bringing up the subject. And later, we had a straight-up, face-to-face discussion about it.

"You go to West Point," they said.

"I don't want to go to West Point."

"You're going," they reiterated. "We've always wanted you to have a formal education. We never had such an opportunity. This is a great opportunity for you."

"I don't want to do it."

"We don't have any money. And you can go to West Point? You better go to West Point."

So I went to West Point. I just did it.

And I went, I think, because of my parents. I believed in them. They had never steered me wrong before. I was on a great team even back then although I didn't completely appreciate it at the time.

And once I got to the academy, even though I wanted to quit many times, I couldn't let my mom and dad down. I could have let myself down, but I couldn't let them down. So I stayed.

Respect for Authority

When my parents were speaking in such stern tones, I respected them even though I didn't necessarily want to hear what they were saying to me. They had never told me to do anything that would hurt me; never given me any advice that might prove detrimental. And at the end of the day, I would always believe my mom.

This is what I want from my players—a belief in a higher authority and respect for that authority. But the truth is that if they don't have it to a certain degree by the time they get to Duke, I'm not sure they'll ever have it.

That's why we try to recruit kids who already show that type of respect. During early meetings, for instance, I'll watch the kids when their parents speak. I'll study their facial expressions and watch their reactions. If a young man rolls his eyes when his mother asks me a question, I'm not sure I'm going to offer him a scholarship. I look for kids who respect their parents because I believe they will have a greater chance of respecting what I say.

All the players on our team must have the discipline to believe and trust in what a coach says to them at a moment's notice—and the coach has to believe and trust in what they say to me at a moment's notice. There is always time pressure on leaders and their teams. In the heat of competition, like during a basketball game, there's simply not enough time to sit down and have a long discussion about what action needs to take place. If a team cannot perform with excellence at a moment's notice, they probably will fail in the long run.

But every leader needs to remember that a healthy respect for authority takes time to develop. It's like building trust. You don't instantly have trust, it has to be earned. One thing it is possible to have instantly, however, is a caring attitude. And I care for every member of my team no matter what happens in their lives—just like my parents cared for me.

In addition to a caring attitude, leaders instill respect for authority by being direct, by communicating regularly, and by being honest. And I was really surprised to learn that all of this was part of the curriculum during my four years at the United States Military Academy.

Honesty and Integrity

West Point was difficult for me, especially the first year. But one of the beauties of the academy was that I always knew where people stood. Nobody ever lied to me because they were prevented from doing so by the West Point honor code: "A cadet will not lie, cheat, or steal—or tolerate those who do." That code was a central part of our four-year experience. And the culture of honesty is a culture I love.

With total honesty, you can cut to the chase quickly. Someone may have an agenda, but at least everyone always knows what it is. Cutting to the chase is big in war, and it's big in competition of any kind—sports, business, you name it.

West Point instilled in me the discipline to tell the truth. And I've tried to implement that same culture with all the basketball teams I've coached. In our business, we have to react

39

quickly. So it's a waste of time to deal with anything less than the truth.

"We can't always take the nice polite way of saying things to each other," I tell all our team members. "We need to communicate in ways that are more direct than most people are used to. We can only do this if we learn to tell the truth, to trust each other, and to understand that we're not trying to hurt each other with our words—even if someone on the outside might think our words are destructive."

This all ties back to having a respect for authority and being able to react at a moment's notice in the heat of competition. Basically, it's "instant belief" in what we say to one another—especially what I say to them. I want our team to know that when I tell them something, it's the truth. They have to know that my word is good. I don't know if there's a bigger issue for me. In the long run, I believe most people will respect and appreciate someone who's honest with them.

Personal Responsibility

I left Chicago for West Point and New York in July of 1965. The academy brochure called the early phase of training "Summer Orientation." And I thought, "Well, that sounds nice." But when I got there, I found out that the cadets called it something else. They called it "Beast Barracks." And for the next two months, they really stripped you of your individual identity. I mean it was pure hell.

The first thing we learned was that we could answer a question in one of only three ways: "Yes, sir," "No, sir," or "No excuse, sir." They've added one since I left: "Sir, I do not understand." I would have used that all the time.

Let me give you an example of an incident that I'll take with me until the day I die—and probably wherever I go after that.

I was walking across an open area with my roommate. We were in our uniforms and we were required to walk in a straight, erect manner.

Well, my roommate stepped in a puddle of water and splashed up a little bit of mud on my shoes. We kept on walking and suddenly I heard the worst word in the world that a plebe can hear.

"Halt!" commanded one of two upperclassmen coming toward us.

"Oh, damn," I thought. "They're not coming over to say 'How ya doin'!'"

Well, these two guys take a look at my roommate and say, "You're okay."

Then they look at me and see my name tag. "What the hell is your name?" one of them asked.

"Krzyzewski, sir."

"What kind of name is that?"

I didn't say anything.

"Well, Mr. Alphabet, or whoever the hell you are, your shoes are cruddy. You're a crudball. How did that happen?"

Now, in real life, 99 percent of the people would want to explain what happened. "Look, we were walking across the area," I wanted to say, "and my knucklehead roommate stepped in a puddle and he got the mud on my shoes. It's not my fault."

But at West Point, that story's not acceptable. So my answer was, "No excuse, sir."

."That's right! You have no excuse! You're a crudball!"

They told my roommate to get going and for the next few minutes one of these upperclassmen just reamed me out. Then he wrote me up and, of course, I received demerits for having mud on my shoes.

So when I finally got back to the dorm, I was angry at my roommate. "Look what you did to me!" I screamed. "Look what happened!"

Well, after a couple more weeks of training, I began to look at that entire incident from a different perspective.

When my roommate stepped in that puddle and splashed mud on my shoes, I had a choice to make. Do I continue or do I go back and change my shoes? What my roommate did was something I had no control over. But the next event was my decision to make. They were my shoes and I was responsible for them. I kept walking and took the chance that I wouldn't be caught. I could have gone back but I didn't. That was my choice. The truth is that I had no right to be mad at my roommate. I should have been mad at myself. And later, when I understood the reality of the situation, I *was* angry with myself. That was a huge lesson for me.

So how does that lesson translate to what I do now as a coach, as a leader?

Well, no matter what happens, it's my team. I'm responsible. There's no excuse. That's how I feel and that's how I act.

And each member of the team, especially the players on the court, have to feel and act the same way. Suppose in a game situation, one of our kids fails to block out a player on a crucial play and the other team scores as a result. Well, we clearly don't want that to happen again, so I might call a timeout and then address the situation in the brief time we have in the huddle. The conversation might go something like this:

"Who had number 52?" I'll ask.

"I did."

"Why didn't you block him out?"

No response.

"Well, are you going to block him out next time?"

"Absolutely."

"You're letting down all these guys by not blocking him out. Do you understand?"

"I understand."

"Don't let us down, okay?"

"Yes, Coach."

There's no time to have an extended conversation or worry about hurting someone's feelings. Now, the individual who didn't block out number 52 should not take my statements to him personally because we have already built up a trusting relationship, because he has a respect for authority, and because he understands the importance of accepting personal responsibility for his actions.

Of course, there may be a reason that our guy didn't block out number 52. It could be that one of the other players didn't do what he was supposed to do. So after the game, we'll review films to see what happened on the court. Then I'll get together with the rest of the team and discuss that particular play. I'll point out what the other guys could have done to better enable this one individual to be in a position to block out number 52.

"If this guy would have forced outside," I'll explain to the team, "instead of letting the ball go to the middle, then Chris wouldn't have had to help out over here, which caused him to be out of position to block number 52. In other words, not

43

everyone did their job. And remember, guys, if one of us fails, we all fail."

In a situation like that, we're not blaming anyone at any time. Rather, we're embracing the hell out of personal responsibility.

This brings me to another couple of valuable lessons I learned during "Beast Barracks." I learned that failure is a part of success and that you can achieve the impossible by depending on your friends.

In our platoon, there were about thirty plebes and we were assigned three to a room. We'd all be outside the barracks dressed in our fatigues when the order would come: "Okay, you've got two minutes to get back here in full dress uniform." Well, there was no way we could get from fatigues to full dress uniforms in two minutes. It was just impossible.

But when the squad leader would yell, "Dismissed!" we'd all run to our rooms and frantically start changing. One guy would be ready first and he'd head out. Then I'd be next and bolt out the door while my other buddy was still changing. We filtered out one by one, we were all late, and we had to get in the late line.

"Why are you late, mister?"

"No excuse, sir."

"That's right, there's no excuse."

But then we were asked other questions.

"Why aren't you out here with your roommates? Why aren't you out here together?"

"No excuse, sir."

"Listen up, mister. If one of you is late, all of you are late. Do you understand that? It's not about you getting out here on time, it's about you and your roommates getting out here on time. If you guys work together, you might make it. So learn to help one another out."

And guess what? Eventually the guys in my room worked together. Eventually, we wouldn't leave our room unless we left together. And you know what else? Because we practiced on working together, we eventually did the impossible—we made it out there in full dress uniform in two minutes. We did it together and we weren't in the late ranks. Individually, it felt good. It felt real good. But collectively, we felt great—I mean GREAT! When they dismissed us, we went back to our room and gave one another high fives. I get goose bumps when I think of it. It was a wonderful lesson—a wonderful shared experience. We learned to depend on one another, which, in turn, made us better.

Through that experience, and many others like it, we learned that failure is just part of success. If you fall down, you get up. If you fail, you try again. If your tent falls down, you put it up again.

We also learned to appreciate the talents of the other guys around us. I never learned how to swim or put up a tent in the inner city of Chicago. So, one of my buddies taught me how to put up a tent because he had been a Boy Scout. Another helped me learn how to swim. Learning to appreciate and depend on one another drew us into relationships—which made us better as a group. It was an add-on to personal responsibility. It was collective responsibility.

When a leader takes responsibility for his own actions and mistakes, he not only sets a good example, he shows a healthy respect for people on his team. I remember, for instance, when Justin Caldbeck was a manager during his freshman year. (He later worked his way onto the basketball team and was a senior in our 1999 run to the Final Four.) We were holding a basketball camp and Justin was handing out drinks. He handed me one and, while walking away, I accidentally dropped my cup to the floor. Justin quickly grabbed a towel and ran over to wipe up.

"Here, Coach, I'll get that," he said.

But I asked him for the towel.

"Here, let me have that, Justin," I said. "When you are the CEO of your own company, I want you to remember that you should still clean up your own mess."

Then I got down on my hands and knees and cleaned the floor.

Discipline Defined

Some people feel that discipline is a dirty word, but it shouldn't be. All it really means is doing what you are supposed to do in the best possible manner at the time you are supposed to do it. And that's not such a bad thing.

But this isn't all about "I love you," and "Let's hold hands and skip." It's also about "Get your rear in gear," "What the hell are you doing?" and "Why aren't you in class?"

We're here for a reason. We're here to get an education and to play basketball. Am I tough on the team? Absolutely. If they don't show respect for the program, for the university, for one another, I'm all over them. I don't want fear to be my primary motivator. But the team has got to know that if they are screwing up, the hammer is going to come down. I'm not going to accept mediocrity at a practice. I'm not going to coach them if they're not giving me their best effort.

So our team has to be disciplined in their work. They have

to participate in a conditioning routine because if they're not physically fit, fatigue sets in early. And when you're tired, you can start making mistakes.

They must also have the discipline of physical habit. Through repetition in practice, we learn some of the basics of basketball. "I've got to be on the help side when the ball's driven. Then I have to rotate. If he gets by, I have to be there to stop him." That sort of thing. And the team has to learn the discipline of physical habit collectively—as a unit.

Then there's the discipline of good sportsmanship, of being patient, of being enthusiastic and energized every time out. I don't want any member of my team to come off the court and throw towels, to sulk at the end of the bench, or to lose their temper.

And, of course, we have to instill the discipline of respect for authority, the discipline of personal responsibility, and the discipline to be honest.

Much of my foundation as a coach, as a leader, as a person, I learned from West Point.

Before I entered the academy, I thought I knew everything. I lived in my own protected little world. My parents had instilled in me a respect for authority and the ability to learn. But West Point took me to another level. I feel that I was very lucky to go there and get a good dose of honesty, honor, and discipline.

Today, I wear my West Point class ring on my left hand—right next to my wedding band. When the center black stone cracked several years ago, I put the ring in a drawer and let it sit. Then, for Christmas, my wife, Mickie, took it out of the drawer and had the special Duke University royal blue gemstone placed in the center.

To me this ring now represents what I want for every one of my players. West Point is the foundation—the structure, the discipline, the respect for authority. And inside, in the center, Duke is the passion and the heart.

Imagine if every person had such a great foundation and then the passion and heart to love what they do. They'd always love their lives.

That's what I call success.

Coach K's Tips

- Leaders instill respect for authority by having a caring attitude, by being direct, by communicating regularly, and by being honest.

- Instill the discipline to tell the truth. It's a waste of time to deal with anything less than the truth.

- Your team needs "instant belief" in what you say to them.

- People have to know that your word is good.

- Embrace the hell out of personal responsibility.

- Failure is part of success.

- Discipline is doing what you are supposed to do in the best possible manner at the time you are supposed to do it.

- Teach good sportsmanship, patience, and the idea that people should be enthusiastic and energized every time out.

- A team has to learn the discipline of physical habit collectively—as a unit.

- If every person has a great foundation and the passion and heart to love what they do, they will always love their life.

4

DYNAMIC LEADERSHIP

"Whatever a leader does now sets up what he does later. And there's always a later."

—Coach K

"My goal has to be worthy of the team's commitment."

—Coach K

"Every season is a journey. Every journey is a lifetime."

—Coach K

*E*very year, we create a brand-new culture for Duke basketball. New people arrive and meld in with the members of the team who have been there for a year or two or three. The older kids become mentors for the freshmen. And sometimes, as we reevaluate our program, many roles change.

Basically, we are a group of people living together over a short period of time in our own culture. How we grow that culture—how we develop communication, how we care for our people—means everything.

In the preseason, I view our organization as land in the Midwest that hasn't yet had much rain. If we experience a deluge of water, the land can't absorb the rain. Instead, it all runs off the surface. The land needs to have moisture daily over a period of time—so the soil can prepare itself. Then, when the storm comes, the land can absorb more water because the soil is stronger and deeper.

Well, it's the same with people.

If our culture is properly developed, if it's nurtured and cared for and watered every day, then in the heat of competition, in those moments when you need to slam home a message, where you need to "spike it," an individual, or the team collectively, will respond well. They'll "soak up" the lesson. And quite often, the entire team will have grown so strong, it appears that each individual is better than they really are.

The course of our year is very much like the seasons of the earth. Similar to spring, in the preseason, things are just beginning to get going. The regular season is like summer when everything is in full growth. The postseason is like autumn. It's beautiful, but we know that the year is going to end. And depending on where you live, autumn can be longer—just as the postseason can be longer if you do well. And finally, for us, the off-season is like winter. Even though the gym is dark, we know the spring is coming. And we begin to prepare for it.

So all year long, the cycle keeps going—always active, always planning, moving, doing. That's the way I view leadership. It never stops. It's going all the time. It's dynamic.

Duke basketball depends on leadership—and I love to lead. It's what I've been doing since I was a kid forming teams on the school playground in Chicago. I'm a coach, and coaching is leading.

Define Your Own Success

When most people think of success, they think of the season ahead and they set a final destination goal. In my line of work, many coaches select winning the national championship as their end goal. But I think that's a pretty shallow view of success—because only one team can win it all.

So if everyone chose that definition of success, then nearly everybody would have an unsuccessful year. I'm also certain that many people out there set that goal because fans and the media tell us that winning the national championship is the only way we'll be successful.

Well, if you're always striving to achieve a success that is defined by someone else, I think you'll always be frustrated. There will never be enough championships. There will never be enough wins. And when you finally attain them, if you're lucky enough to do so, they'll only be numbers. Somebody will say you were great or that you were successful, but ultimately you'll know it's an empty success.

The only way to get around such an unhappy ending is to continually define your own success. And it begins in the pre-season before everything bursts into full bloom. Your definition of success should have more depth than the equivalent of winning a national championship. It should be whatever passion moves you deep in your heart.

My passion is to coach and do things to the best of my ability. I want our team to get better every day. If we can do that, the other stuff will take care of itself. And I also have a quiet personal goal to be consistently excellent. Every time we go out on the court, I want us to play the perfect game. Every time we play a game, I want it to be a masterpiece.

I work with our team to help achieve that goal. But I don't tell the other members of my team that every game has to be a masterpiece. That's one of the reasons I call it a "quiet" goal. If I were to tell them, it might put on extra pressure. They may think they'll have to do everything with perfection. I try not to put pressure on their performance. I want them to love their performance. When they step out on the court, I want them to boldly go in the direction of their abilities—with intelligence. And I want every member of the team to think, "I can do this."

A good leader has to look beyond what his team is doing now—or there could be serious consequences down the road. Whatever a leader does now sets up what he does later. And there's always a later.

Planning and Preparation

Every leader has to look ahead at the entire season. They have to plan and prepare for every phase, and then remain flexible when things don't go exactly according to plan. Every long-term strategy must be adjustable and people on the team must be prepared accordingly.

In the case of Duke basketball, we consider what would happen if there are injuries, lack of growth in one individual, or greater-than-expected growth in another. I call this ability to adjust "running motion offense," which simply means that we don't have a set play. Rather, each time down the court, we evaluate the situation. What does this look like? How can I attack now? It's important to have a long-term strategy, but no one should be a slave to their plan.

When I hear the quote "There are a lot of people who want to win, but winners prepare to win," I think of Coach Bob Knight. I played under him for four years at Army and he gave me the opportunity to be an assistant with him at Indiana. He also recommended me for the head coaching job at Duke.

And I'll never forget what Coach Knight did for me when my father died unexpectedly of a cerebral hemorrhage in

1969, my senior year at West Point. I had just been given the game ball after our big win over Navy when my brother, Bill, called with the bad news. For me, my dad's death was like a bolt out of the blue. Even though he had been ill for some time, I was unaware because the family did not want anything to disturb my time at the academy.

Coach Knight drove me to the airport early in the morning and I got on a flight and went home. He came out later that evening and spent a couple of days with my family. That really helped my mom and me a lot—and I was very grateful and appreciative.

I also remember being concerned about our two remaining basketball games against Colgate and Rochester. If we won them both, we would have a chance to go to the NIT (National Invitation Tournament). Even though I was his captain and lead ball handler, Coach Knight was more concerned about me than those two ball games. "Take all the time you need, Mike," he said. "Come back only when you're ready."

I flew back just in time for the games—and we won them both and made it to the NIT. That was the year my buddies at West Point took up a collection to bring my mom out to the final four of the tournament. But because she wasn't yet quite up to the trip, they took the money and bought her a West Point rocking chair. My mom treasured that rocker for the rest of her life.

Bob Knight had a big influence on me. He's a brilliant man, an outstanding coach. From him, I learned many of the basic strategies of basketball that I apply every day during the season. He taught me that there are no magic wands, that you have to succeed by working hard as a group. And I also learned a great deal about organization and preparation from Coach Knight.

Success is not a matter of just wanting to win. It's a matter of preparing to win—which is much more important. Now, if you can combine the two, you're on the right road. But the preparation to win is paramount to future success.

In general, we try to bring our team along game by game so that we're playing well at the end of the season. We want to be the best we can be in March. And I'm always careful to make sure that we don't start out too strong or peak too soon. It would be like starting a mile run with a 100 yard dash.

I look at the entire year. It has to be carefully planned and it has to be reacted to. Actually, I look at the year in segments of time and plan out our schedule of games accordingly. In the first month of the season, we may put the team through some tough situations—play in a tournament and compete against a few really tough teams. And maybe we'll set up a challenging stretch around Thanksgiving. Then, during our exam break in late December, we'll pause to reflect on what happened and how well we performed. Next, we'll look at the coming segment of the season and adjust as necessary.

The season is so long, we have to create a series of objectives to strive for. It can be a series of games or anything that makes sense. I like to call it an energy cycle. In order to keep a team motivated over an extended interval of time, planned short bursts of energy like this can be very effective.

In 1999, for instance, I scheduled our team to play a late-January game against St. John's University in Madison Square Garden—three days before we played North Carolina, our archrival. I could have left the schedule alone and given the team those three extra days for rest and preparation. But I was thinking ahead to the NCAA tournament. So I told our players that the four-day period that encompassed the St. John's and North Carolina games would be a simulation of what we might experience in March. The St. John's game would be like an East Regional championship game—complete with the atmosphere of a vast arena and thousands of fans. Besides that, I knew St. John's would be a great team, probably ranked in the top ten nationally. They'd be a big test for us. Then we'd have to turn around right away and play another top-ranked team in North Carolina—which I said would be like going to the Final Four.

"This is the type of thing we're going to have to go through if we are to have a chance at winning the national championship," I told the players. "We might as well start getting the feel for what it will be like."

The whole thing kind of reminds me of when I was back on the schoolyard playground with my eight- and nine-year-old pals. "Okay, I'm a Chicago Cub today. Number 14, Ernie Banks, comes to the plate. Bottom of the ninth, score tied. He hits it. It's outta here! Yay!"

It's imagination. It's fun. It worked when I was a kid. And I believe it still works today.

By the way, we did win the East Regional championship game against Temple University that year and, as a result, went to the Final Four. And I reminded the team about that big game in late January against St. John's that we won in overtime. And then how we went on to defeat North Carolina a few days later.

"*Remember* how the simulation felt, guys," I said. "Because *this* is the real thing."

Shared Goals

Goals are important in leadership. They should be realistic, they should be attainable, and they should be shared among all members of the team. Some people use the term "common" goals. But I prefer the word "shared" because it's uncommon to have shared goals.

Shared goals suggest more depth. They suggest that you are going to cooperate with one another, that a bond will develop. And when two people have a strong bond with each other, they both give equally. With a strong bond, not all the giving is done by the leader alone.

In the preseason, I suggest goals in order to reach my own personal objective of forging better bonds among the team. I may indicate to a senior like Chris Carrawell that one of his goals should be to build a close relationship with incoming freshman point guard Jason Williams. Jason will need strength on the court and Chris can provide that for him if they have a strong bond.

In the early 1990s, I did that with Bobby Hurley, Christian Laettner, and Grant Hill. When Grant was a freshman, I told Bobby and Christian that this kid was special. "He's such a good guy," I told them, "that he's going to be polite and stand in line because he respects authority. Well he's too good a player to stand in line. He'll look at you two guys and he'll think, 'It's *their* team.' I want you two to pull him in, build a bond with him, and make him know that this is his team, too."

By involving Hurley and Laettner, I was showing that I had a lot of confidence in them both. And I knew that they could bring Hill further along than just me working with him one on one.

Hurley and Laettner accepted my suggestion and rose to the occasion. They and Grant Hill became close friends and spent many hours together. And all that bonding translated into tremendous teamwork and success on the court. The bond those three guys formed was tremendous. They were the core of the 1991 team that won the NCAA tournament. In essence, that early conversation I had with them impacted the entire team.

There are teams that form stronger bonds than others. Because these three guys were so tight, I knew in the preseason that this group had a chance to win the national championship. At a certain point, I told the team that they had the potential to win it all. But it wasn't something I talked about frequently. And I did not say that if we won a certain number of games, we'd take it all.

Actually, I never have a goal that involves number of wins—never. It would just tend to limit our potential. Suppose, for instance, that I say our goal for the coming year is to win twenty games and go to the NCAA tournament. If the team wins twenty games and makes the tournament, is that the end of it?

Rather, I worked with the 1991 team to set a couple of goals that had nothing to do with winning ball games. I say "worked with the team" because every team, in part, dictates what goals are set. After all, they are the ones who are going to have to achieve the goals. Our goals revolve around playing together so we can be good every time out.

"This team can really be the best defensive team we've ever had," I said to the 1991 group. "That's got to be one of our goals." Notice I did not specifically mention winning or losing ball games. However, if a team works at becoming the best defensive team possible, they will put themselves in a position to win every ball game. And I believe, over the course of the year, they'll win more games than if a number, say twenty, was set as the goal.

After the 1991 team won the NCAA tournament, I immediately took a different approach with the 1992 team. When we returned to Duke, I got everybody together. "Next year," I announced, "we're going to have our own championship rings made—and on them it will say 'back-to-back national championships'!" Hoots and hollers went up as they all started thinking about next year's possibilities.

I also told this team that one of our goals for the year would be to play hard all the time. "You don't have that Duke uniform on, and you don't cross those lines on the court unless you're going to play hard together. I'll back you guys all the way if you play hard together."

Playing hard together, being the best defensive team, and players building strong bonds with one another, are shared goals that involve working together as a group over the entire year. If a team consistently concentrates on goals like that, major achievements happen.

I think it's also important to remember that if circumstances change during the year, goals might have to change as well. In addition, progress has to be monitored on a regular basis and good work has to be rewarded and encouraged. When I saw that Hurley and Laettner were making a lot of progress with Hill, for instance, I gave them a pat on the back. "Bobby, Christian, what a great job you're doing with Grant," I told them. "Way to go."

The commitment those guys put into that relationship was remarkable. And the goal itself was deserving of the effort they put forth. That's another principle I think about when setting goals. It's the idea that *my goal has to be worthy of the team's commitment.* This is a tenet we were taught at West Point— and it is one I think about often, especially when I reflect on the Vietnam War.

My first assignment after graduation in 1969 was as a field artillery officer at Fort Carson, Colorado. That took me to 1971 when I was on orders for Vietnam. But because of the massive troop pullout, I was sent to Korea.

Some of my classmates lost their lives fighting in Vietnam. They were great guys. They loved their country. And, like all of us at the academy, they were taught to win. But it became clear that the powers that be were not trying to win the Vietnam War. So my friends, who were fully committed, had a regulator put on them.

I never want to be part of something like that. I never want to lead a team that doesn't have a clear definition of where they are headed or are not allowed the full freedom to pursue what's in their hearts. If you're a leader, you'd better understand that if you want people on your team who are fully committed, then you'd better be fully committed to a course of action that allows proper use of that commitment. If not, you should change your course of action. In other words, your goal must be worthy of your team's commitment.

I have friends with whom I went to school who are buried at West Point cemetery. I'll never forget that. So if I ask an eighteen-year-old on my team for his full commitment, I'm going to make certain that wherever I'm leading him, both the destination and the journey will be worthy.

Every Season Is a Journey

I look at each year in basketball as an integral part of life. Every season is a journey. Every journey is a lifetime.

Nobody can predict what's going to happen along the way. Some bad things may occur, some great things may come to pass. But whatever happens, like life, the journey should be enjoyed. We ought to soak up the moisture that falls daily—

and not allow ourselves to get bogged down in our original plan without adjusting to whatever occurs along our path. That way, we look forward to success on a year-to-year basis.

During the season, your team should be led with exuberance and excitement.

You should live the journey.

You should live it right.

You should live it together.

You should live it shared.

You should try to make one another better.

You should get on one another if somebody's not doing their part.

You should hug one another when they are.

You should be disappointed in a loss and exhilarated in a win.

It's all about the journey.

It should be honest and it should be real.

It's not about winning games or what other people's expectations of us may be. We're not going to fall into the traps that so many people fall into. That's not why we're going to play. We're going to play for innocence.

I'm ready. There are no excuses. Let's go!

COACH K's TIPS

- If your culture is properly developed, then in the heat of competition, when you have to slam home a message, an individual or the team will respond well.

- If you're always striving to achieve success that is defined by someone else, you'll always be frustrated. Define your own success.

- Whatever a leader does now sets up what he does later. And there's always a later.

- Every long-term strategy must be adjustable, and people on the team must be prepared accordingly. Teach them to adjust.

- Success is a matter of preparing to win.

- Goals should be realistic, attainable, and shared among all members of the team.

- Never set a goal that involves number of wins—never. Set goals that revolve around playing together as a team. Doing so will put you in a position to win every game.

- Progress has to be monitored on a regular basis, and good work has to be rewarded and encouraged.

- Every goal has to be worthy of the team's commitment.

- If you're not fully committed to a course of action that allows use of your team's full commitment, then change your course of action.

- Every season is a journey. Live it with exuberance and excitement. Live it right.

REGULAR SEASON

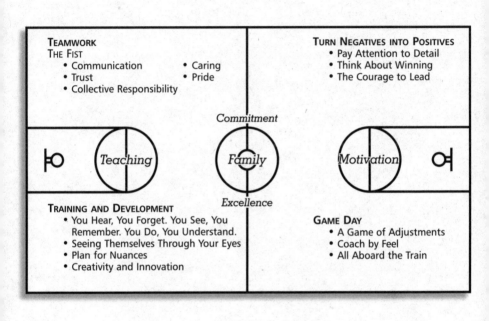

TEAMWORK
THE FIST
- Communication
- Trust
- Collective Responsibility
- Caring
- Pride

TURN NEGATIVES INTO POSITIVES
- Pay Attention to Detail
- Think About Winning
- The Courage to Lead

Commitment

Teaching

Family

Motivation

Excellence

TRAINING AND DEVELOPMENT
- You Hear, You Forget. You See, You Remember. You Do, You Understand.
- Seeing Themselves Through Your Eyes
- Plan for Nuances
- Creativity and Innovation

GAME DAY
- A Game of Adjustments
- Coach by Feel
- All Aboard the Train

"There are five fundamental qualities that make every team great: communication, trust, collective responsibility, caring, and pride. I like to think of each as a separate finger on the fist. Any one individually is important. But all of them together are unbeatable."

—COACH K

5

TEAMWORK

"You develop a team to achieve what one person cannot accomplish alone. All of us *alone* are weaker, by far, than if all of us are *together*."

—**Coach K**

"Confidence shared is better than confidence only in yourself."

—**Coach K**

"Confrontation simply means meeting the truth head-on."

—**Coach K**

*A*ll right, hold up, you guys," I say calmly as I interrupt practice, stride onto the court, and single out Brian Davis. "Brian, you know what? We're going to have a big operation right now."

"What's that, Coach?"

"We're going to remove *your* head from *your* rear end right now."

Suddenly, you can hear a pin drop in the gymnasium as all the players stare at me with grim faces.

"Now, you can help me with the operation or I can do it alone. It's your choice. But in the next thirty seconds, your head better be out of your rear end. Do you understand?"

"Yes, sir," replies Davis.

"You're catching the ball and *then* you're getting ready to make a move. You should not do that in stages. It should be done in one fluid motion. It's called 'thinking.' Right now, you catch the ball and then you think. I want you to be thinking as you're catching it. Do you understand?"

"Yes, Coach."

"Your head has to be in the ball game *all the time.* You have to concentrate *all the time.* Okay, let's try it a couple of times."

As we run the drill with all the players watching intently at Davis's progress, Brian starts to get it right.

"Good! Now you're thinking!" I exclaim. "Do you know how much better a player you are when you think? I love who you are when you think. I want you to be a good basketball player all the time. Is that what you want?"

"Yes."

"Well, then, *think!* Think *all the time.*"

Later in the practice—it could be two minutes or twenty minutes later—when Brian makes a good catch of the ball, I'll interrupt again—only this time I'll praise him.

"Yes! Unbelievable! Did we get that on tape? The operation was a success! Brian, how does it feel to have your head out of your rear end and moving freely?" Now all the guys are laughing and Brian has a big smile on his face.

After practice, *I know exactly* what is going to happen. The players will gather around Davis in the locker room. "Hey, Brian," someone will say, "Coach was pretty rough on you."

"Yeah, but he was right," Brian will respond. "I wasn't catching the ball properly. I had my head up my rear."

And one of the freshmen might say, "My high school coach never did anything like that."

"Well, you're not in high school anymore," Brian will fire back. "You should want the coach to correct your mistakes. You should want him to make you better—because when you get better, we all get better."

I knew *exactly* what was going to happen with the "head-out-of-your-rear-end" incident because I had set it up prior to the practice. I had a pact with Brian Davis that went something like this: "If I get on you, you can't show even the slightest hint that you knew it was coming. And when you get back in the locker room, you can't call me an SOB. In return, you'll be helping me teach the team something—and they'll see *your* strength."

Brian agreed to the deal because he was a leader on our team. In fact, he was one of the team captains on our 1991–1992 team. He already had a certain amount of trust and credibility built up with the younger guys because he was one of the guys. It was an effective teaching tool for me because it was not just the head coach telling the team something, it was the team telling the team.

The Fist

I look at the members of our team like the five fingers of a hand. Some hands have small fingers that easily come together as a fist. Other hands have very large fingers but, if they never come together as a fist, they probably won't be as powerful as the smaller hand that does. In other words, if five talented individuals don't perform as a team, they may not be as strong as five less-talented individuals who do.

Any one fist can break any one finger. Therefore, my goal as a leader is to create a dominant team where all five fingers fit together into a powerful fist.

In general, I want to constantly improve so that we will be at our best during the last stages of the regular season. To make that happen, I try to create an identity of teamwork. As soon as the team achieves a group *mentality*, it can assume a group *identity*. Then, any combination of five players can play as one.

There are also five fundamental *qualities* that make every team great: *communication, trust, collective responsibility, caring,* and *pride*. I like to think of each as a separate finger on the fist. Any one individually is important. But all of them together are unbeatable.

"You develop a team to achieve what one person cannot accomplish alone," I frequently tell the players. "All of us *alone* are weaker, by far, than if all of us are *together.*"

It's the easiest thing in the world to understand, but the hardest thing to achieve. So in order to make it happen, the team has to *learn* how to think as one. We may not always be able to beat a team physically, but we should be able to out-think the other guy.

Thinking is one of the toughest things a leader has to teach. To be able to think on the run has been a key to Duke basketball success.

Communication

People learn how to think by communicating. So in our program, we not only employ an offensive system and a defensive system—we employ a communication system.

Effective communication—the first quality of the fist—is manifested in talk. But all too often, people take talking for granted. Around the coffee bar, at the lunch table, or in the locker room, people are always talking to one another. But leaders should not assume that people are going to talk to one another when they are performing their jobs. As a matter of fact, in business, an employee is less likely to talk to a member of the team when he's doing his job than when he's on a break.

Leaders have to remind people to talk to one another. They have to teach people to talk. And believe it or not, at Duke, we teach players to talk through repetition—just like other physical drills in practice. Let me give you a couple of examples.

In an individual drill, for instance, where a coach is teaching defensive footwork, we may set up an imaginary situation where we tell the player that the coach has the ball and one of his teammates is covering the coach. The player then talks to that imaginary teammate as he's practicing his defensive footwork: "You're okay, you're okay. I got help here. I got help here. Watch screen, watch screen. Stay out, I'm inside now." We also ask the player to call for the ball during an individual shooting drill. If he gets in the habit of yelling for the ball, his hands will instantly go up in a reflex motion. And then, once a player has the ball, his teammates may see that he's open before he himself realizes it. So they would yell, "Shot! Shot! Take the shot!"

We practice these drills over and over again so that the players get into the familiar role of talking. Once they step onto the court, there are two natural instincts that have to be overcome. First of all, it's like entering a classroom, where the players are used to the rule that they must be quiet. Second, when people are in a pressure situation, there is a tendency to think quietly and talk to themselves. We don't want them to be quiet or to talk to themselves. We want them to talk and think out loud. The whole idea is to communicate well during a game situation. Because during a game, the players have to react instantly. We simply don't have the time to stop and call a meeting to determine what we want to do next.

We have to be on our toes every minute, every second. It's just like any hot company whose leaders don't have time to stop and deliberate. They have to adjust while on the run so they don't miss any great scoring opportunities.

So I counsel our players to get their heads together in the huddle during breaks in the action. And the players all have an understanding among themselves that during the huddle, whether it's in practice or in a game, there's no BS—only the truth can be spoken. Whether something's going wrong or something's going right, they need to talk to each other right away—as soon as they see something. That way, if things aren't going well, corrections are made immediately. And, conversely, if someone's really got it running smoothly, they are complimented and encouraged by the others—or they themselves share the secret of their success. I've always believed that confidence shared is better than confidence only in yourself.

I also want our players to talk in the huddle because they might notice something that I cannot see from the sidelines. Coaches have a different view than the players. So they must allow the leaders in the arena to make an adjustment, or call an "audible" if the need arises. And during a timeout, that player can also inform the head coach so that a different course of action can be pursued.

I think it pays for a leader to ask a player's advice during those extended timeouts. It's easier to do with veteran teams because they're more experienced. But it works with young teams, too, because when a head coach asks a player for advice, it gives that player immense credibility, which, in turn, makes the entire team stronger. Communication like this permeates through the entire group. It's not only the coach communicating, it's everybody communicating.

Many leaders in business hire people solely for their technical merits. "Gotta have a guy who can make the sale." "Gotta have a guy who can keep the books." But, sometimes, in the accomplishment of his job, a person who is self-centered becomes an island—where they don't care about other members of the team. Well, at Duke, I may not recruit a guy just because he shoots 90 percent from the free throw line. I'd rather have an 80 percent free throw shooter who will talk to his teammates than I would a 90 percent free throw shooter who is an island to himself on the team.

Billy King, a great Duke basketball player (and National Defensive Player of the Year in 1988), had enormous status even though he wasn't the best field goal or free throw shooter on the team. However, he was a great defender, he really understood the game, and he was one of the best communicators I ever had the privilege of coaching. Billy King was equal to or better than anyone else on the team status-wise because, in our system, communication is just as important as technical ability.

It was just as easy for Billy King to communicate as it was for Johnny Dawkins to hit a jump shot. So every year, I search for the communicator on the team—just like I try to find the guy with heart.

Trust

In leadership, there are no words more important than trust. In any organization, trust must be developed among every member of the team if success is going to be achieved. That's why I make it a point to be certain that our players always know I'm going to be straight with them.

"Fellas, I am the truth," I will say to every team. "At any time, I can and will tell you where you stand and how you're doing. I'll tell you what you're doing right and I'll tell you when you're screwing up." In addition, every member of the team knows right up front not only that I will tell them the truth—but I will do so *as soon as possible.*

I have never been a memo guy. I like to speak to people in person. But face-to-face communication is not something that is practiced regularly in most organizations. As a matter of fact, it is often avoided—especially in business. Many managers don't like to deal with confrontation—which, unfortunately, has the same negative connotation as "discipline" or "work." People are not truthful and open with each other simply because the truth is often the most difficult pill to swallow for the person receiving it. It's also often difficult to express for the person delivering it.

I believe, however, that confrontation is good.

Straightforward face-to-face communication is usually done to overcome some sort of obstacle—a fear or a lack of confidence, for example. A leader does not beat those things by just hugging them or letting them go.

If Johnny Dawkins missed four shots in a row during a key game, I would call him over and say something to him. "Johnny, next time down, I want you to take another shot. Be confident. You're going to make the next shot."

I don't want a kid to carry any baggage forward. Each play is new.

In truth, I was always reminding Johnny Dawkins to believe that his fifth shot was his first shot. And it's the same in business. If a company's best salesperson has just come in second place four straight times, should the supervisor ignore it? Should he say, "Thanks for coming in second"? Or should he sit down and offer the salesperson some encouragement and confidence? "Look, I know you're better than that. I don't want you to be discouraged. Don't fear for your job, because I'm behind you. I want you to go back out there and give it your best shot again. Your fifth shot is your first shot."

A face-to-face situation like this is just as much a confrontation as anything else. In fact, confrontation simply means meeting the truth head-on. Besides, true friends will tell each other tough things.

For leaders in a high-paced environment, it's absolutely critical to deal with any issue in a rapid manner—especially if the problem has the potential to bring down the level of performance of the team. If leaders don't deal with a slump in performance, or any other form of nonperformance, the organization is not going to achieve its goals. And in a case like that, it's the company beating the company—not the competition beating the company.

Well, I don't ever want to be in a situation where Duke is beating Duke. That's why I want my teams to be tough enough to deal with face-to-face communication. But we're able to be successful at it only because we trust one another. We work hard to focus on the truth, look one another in the eye, and then take action for the good of the team. And once the confrontation is done, it's done. The bond is not jeopardized, because ours is a relationship based on trust.

Collective Responsibility

I will never forget a game in 1989 when Danny Ferry was a senior. Duke was playing Arizona in a hotly contested, very close game at the Meadowlands in New Jersey—which has always been a special place in my coaching career. All the players had poured their hearts into this particular game and it went right down to the wire.

With just one second left, Christian Laettner, then a freshman, was fouled and sent to the free throw line to shoot one-and-one. We were down by only two points, 77–75, so if he hit the first shot, he'd get a second shot to tie the game. However, if he missed the front end of the one-and-one, he would not get a second shot and we would lose the ball game.

All eyes were on Christian as he stood by himself at the free throw line and took his first shot. The ball hit the back of the rim and bounced out. Arizona got the rebound, and we lost the game.

As the buzzer sounded, our senior captains, Danny Ferry and Quin Snyder, rushed over to Laettner and put their arms around the dejected freshman. And then the rest of the team went up to console him. I was especially proud of Danny because he was a candidate for National Player of the Year—which eventually went to Sean Elliott of Arizona. If we had won that game, Danny might have received the award. But there was no selfishness at that moment from any member of our team. As a matter of fact, I distinctly recall Quin Snyder saying, "Laett, don't worry about it, man. We win and we lose together."

For me, that moment when the team rallied around Christian was better than winning any national championship. It was one of the best examples of collective responsibility I have ever witnessed. And I didn't have to initiate anything. I didn't say, "Hey, guys, go out and help Christian." I just watched.

People are going to step in mud puddles. They are going to make mistakes. If you are going to have a great team, there should be no excuses and no finger-pointing when somebody

77

else on your team is not perfect. Because when you point blame at someone else, one finger sticks out—and you no longer have a fist. Besides, that one finger can easily be broken off.

Some people like to win individually and some like to lose selectively. They'll say, "It's someone else's responsibility," or "It's not my fault." But one of the key components of keeping that fist together is taking responsibility for your actions as a team. Every individual member has to realize that it's *our* job no matter what happens.

This is the bottom line: We win or we lose together. Great teams embrace responsibility. It's that simple.

Caring

The conclusion of the 1989 Arizona game was also a good illustration of the fourth quality of the fist—*caring*.

When the guys on the bench rushed out to Laettner after the buzzer sounded, it showed how much they cared about Christian. They cared about him as a person, a friend, a player, and as a teammate. And that encouragement impacted Christian's performance for the remainder of his career. For the rest of 1989 alone, he hit 90 percent of his free throws.

He was able to put that early loss behind him, in part not only because of the hugs he received, but because of what he saw in his teammates' eyes. If, after a failure, a group of people are always able to look at one another and see compassion and empathy in one another's eyes, then they are going to be looking at a winning team.

My wife, Mickie, frequently reminds me to have a different player over to the house each week for a session of individual instruction or for just a conversation. No matter how busy I am, or perceive myself to be, I need to make time for that kind of personal attention. It reinforces that we're all part of a family. Nothing demonstrates that you care about people more than spending personal time with them. And the more it's a one-on-one encounter, the better.

The concept of caring, however, is not singular in description.

It's more than "I care about you as a person." It's also about "I care about the job I'm doing on the basketball court." It's caring about the individual, caring about the team, caring about the team's performance, caring about *high* performance, about excellence. And it's caring about winning—about being the best you can be.

That's also caring. And *that* kind of caring spurs people to take action. It causes people to work harder, to get off their duffs and move. "I'm going to do this because I *care* about my job and because I *care* about the people I work with."

In no small way, *caring* can be a powerful motivational factor on any team.

Pride

My mom always gave her best in everything she did even if it was something as simple as making a batch of chocolate chip cookies. When we were a little poorer, she put three chips in every cookie. Later on, there were four chips. But if a cookie had only two chips in it, it wasn't her cookie. Whatever she put her signature on, it was done right.

From that simple lesson, I've taken the principle that:

"Everything we do has our own personal signature on it. So we want to do it as well as we possibly can."

That's called *pride*—the fifth quality of the fist.

When I played basketball as a point guard for Bob Knight at West Point, the ball I was passing to another player did not have written on it "Wilson" (the name of the manufacturer). As far as I was concerned, the name written on that ball was "Krzyzewski." If it was not a good pass, I'd be responsible for it. And when it *was* a good pass, the guy I was throwing it to had better catch it. Also, if there was a loose ball on the court, it didn't say "Wilson" on it, it said "Krzyzewski." So I dove for every loose ball like it was my own personal property.

As a coach, whenever I feel that our basketball team is not showing enough pride in their work—whenever they're not diving for that loose ball, or jumping for that loose rebound—I will pause to tell the story about an incident that happened to my mother when she was seventy-five years old.

One afternoon, Mom got off a bus in Chicago and was walking home when three teenage boys attacked her and tried to take away her purse. Now, in a situation like that, most women would let go and not risk a confrontation. "Here, take it all and leave me alone," they'd probably say.

Not my mother.

She held on to her purse with a vise grip—because it was hers. And after a few moments, those kids realized that this little old lady was *not* going to let go and they were *not* going to get that purse—so they ran off.

After I relate that story, I'll turn to the team and say something like: "Now, guys, if a seventy-five-year-old lady is going to fight for her purse, you nineteen- and twenty-year-olds *aren't* going to fight for a loose ball? You can't grab a rebound? C'mon! You should all be ashamed of yourselves. We're not going to be a good team until we have enough pride to believe that when a ball is loose on the court, it's *Duke's* ball. When you make a pass, it says 'Amaker' on it. When the ball goes up in the air and the shot misses, it says 'Alarie' on it. When there's a loose ball near Shane, the ball has 'Battier' written on it."

When *everyone* on our team believes that our own personal signature is on *everything* our team does—then we have a chance to be a great basketball team. And not until we believe that every ball we play with says "Duke" on it, will we be proud of our performance.

When it comes to effective teamwork, the fist—with its five qualities of communication, trust, collective responsibility, caring, and pride—is more important than anything. It's more important than technical expertise, for instance.

Many leaders concentrate on only technical aspects of their profession. In basketball, it's "We have to be in shape," "We have to run good plays," "We have to be good defensively." And all that is important. A leader has to be sure all of those things are done. But all the technical aspects of the game are better achieved if the fist is clenched tight.

The fist is also more important than individual skill and talent. A small company with moderate talent that works together can outperform a medium-size company with great talent that acts separately. And a $4 billion company with a lot of talent acting individually can become a $10 billion company when that same talent acts collectively as a team.

But leaders must be constantly monitoring the team's fist to make sure it's strong and tight. If that fist begins to open up—and *then* you get into competition—one of the fingers can be broken off and the team can lose the game.

A leader should never assume that the fist is secure—because it's impacted by all the things that impact people. Somebody's wife may be having a baby or a miscarriage. A relative may be ill. There may be a death in the family. There's a fire. These are things that leaders may not normally think about. But they are just as important to be concerned with as a person's skill at doing his job.

When a team is working well together—when the members are clenched tight like a fist—a moment of weakness by any individual will be compensated for by the rest of the group. When one finger is weak, the other four stay firm and hold the weak link in tight. And I'm not talking about only when you're in competitive situations, I'm talking about all situations.

Suppose several kids on our basketball team are at a party at two o'clock in the morning on a Saturday night. Suppose there's some drinking and all of a sudden some drugs come out. Maybe one of the kids has a moment of weakness and is tempted. But if the others notice what's going on (and they should if they're a true team), they can be strong for their friend and say, "No, that stuff's not for us, let's get out of here."

And even if a kid is alone in a situation like that, just knowing that he's a member of our team will make him stop and think twice because he knows there are others depending on *him*. One of my goals in establishing teamwork is always to get the team believing that they are part of something bigger than themselves.

A *good* player usually knows when he has talent. But a *great* player realizes that he can achieve greatness only if he has other good players around him. Michael Jordan understood that he needed guys on his team like Scottie Pippen and

John Paxson. Smokey Robinson wouldn't have been as good in the early stages of his development if he didn't have the Miracles on stage with him. He needed his team to attain a certain level so that he could eventually go out on his own and become even greater.

When it comes to my philosophy surrounding teamwork, I have a simple, straightforward saying that I pass on to anyone who will listen: Two are better than one if two act as one. And if you believe that two acting as one are better than one, just imagine what an entire team acting as one can do.

Coach K's Tips

- Any one fist can break any one finger. Therefore, your goal as a leader should be to create a dominant team where all five fingers fit together into a powerful fist.

- Adjust while you're on the run so that you don't miss any great scoring opportunities.

- A confidence shared is better than a confidence only in yourself.

- Don't hire people solely on their technical merits. Consider whether they can work in a team environment.

- Communication skills are just as important as technical skills.

- Always search for the communicator on the team.

- In leadership, no word is more important than trust.

- Confrontation is good. It simply means meeting the truth head-on.

- Teach the principle that "Your fifth shot is your first shot."

- Great teams embrace responsibility.

- Win or lose together.

- Caring is a powerful motivational force on any team.

- Believe that the loose ball you're chasing has your name on it.

- Two are better than one if two act as one.

6

TRAINING AND DEVELOPMENT

"It's not what *I know,* it's what *they do* on the court that really matters."

—Coach K

"If you put a plant in a jar, it will take the shape of the jar. But if you allow the plant to grow freely, twenty jars might not be able to hold it."

—Coach K

"We won championships at Duke because of what happened behind closed doors."

—Christian Laettner (1988–1992)

*T*he score is 72–69. Visitors are ahead. They have one free throw to shoot. And there are 48 seconds left in the game.

If they hit the shot, we'll be two possessions down. If they miss it, we'll be only one three-point possession down, two two-point possessions.

The ball is inbounded. The visiting player misses the shot. Roshown McLeod grabs the rebound and fires it to Steve Wojciechowski.

What's Wojo going to do at this point? I wonder. Is he going to rush for the three-point shot or is he going to set up a lower-risk two-pointer and then use the clock to try and get the ball back? No need to call a timeout, I'm thinking. The team looks strong and focused. So I'll watch what happens.

Wojo gets the ball and charges down the court with a ferocious intent. Just by looking at the expression on his face, I can tell what he's thinking and what he's going to do. "Got to

make the shot. Got to make the shot. Must hit this three."
Wojo makes no passes, gets to the three-point line, fires, and
misses. A visiting player gets the rebound and is immediately
fouled to stop the clock. Now we're in a worse situation and
there are 10 fewer seconds on the clock.

"All right, hold it!" I say.

I've been standing behind the basket during this practice
simulation and I now stride out to the foul line and call everybody over.

"Wojo, what were you thinking on that play?"

"Well, I was thinking that I had to make a three-pointer. I
was thinking I want to win."

"I know you want to win, son. But there are more ways to
win than you just running down the court and taking a three."

Then I relate a military example.

"A machine gun is on the hill. You and your men are
pinned down below. You have to take out the machine gun.
But if you charge up that hill by yourself and say, 'I want to
win,' the machine gun will probably mow you down, right?"

"Right."

"So you die. But you say, 'Well, it was okay because I tried
to win'? I say, 'Baloney.' You're dead and we're worse off as a
group now than we were before, aren't we?"

"Yeah, we are."

"So how do you get the machine gun out," I'll ask rhetor-
ically. "Well, maybe you go around the side of the hill. Maybe
you involve the rest of your platoon. You might call for a di-
versionary military barrage or you might even call the air force
in to drop a bomb. There are numerous ways to take out that
machine gun without getting yourself killed and putting your
team in a worse hole than they're already in.

"Understand, Wojo? Does everybody understand?"

As heads nod affirmatively in unison, I walk back behind the basket and say: "Okay, let's do it again."

You Hear, You Forget. You See, You Remember. You Do, You Understand.

Wojo's gamelike simulation is a perfect example of how I view training and development. During our practice sessions, I strive to prepare the team to act well during a real game. In short, I train them to be effective.

The overriding concept I employ in teaching revolves around this simple phrase: "You hear, you forget. You see, you remember. You do, you understand."

How much I speak to the players on our team is important, but they'll forget a lot of what they *hear*. It's also important to make sure they watch and observe through action and videotape. Usually, the team will remember more of what they *see*. But the most critical aspect of our team training is what the guys actually *do* and what they *understand*.

So we perform all kinds of gamelike drills over and over again. Such repetition is designed to refine physical habits. And it is key to ensuring that a team will perform well in a real-life situation—because the group will not only hear and see what we tell them, they'll actually execute what we tell them.

Whenever I have a practice session with my team, I go in fully prepared. I put together a one-page handwritten lesson. I decide not only what *points* I want to get across, I also pick different *places* where I will talk to them—in the locker room, in the middle of the court, on the bench, under the basket, and so on. I choose a variety of spots in order to change the environment so the guys will stay attuned and aware. That way they'll be more likely to retain some of the things I tell them.

I also determine how *long* I will talk to the team. If I have a seven-minute drill planned, I can't take four minutes to explain it. And while I don't want to rush my explanation, I want to get it done in about a minute so that they spend six minutes "doing" rather than only "hearing."

At every practice, I want our team to play hard, play smart, and play together. Most groups don't play hard all the time—just like most people don't work hard all the time. But the single most intimidating element of competition, aside from raw talent, is a team working and playing hard for the entire game. "Here they come again! These guys just keep coming! What are they going to do this time? What are *we* going to do this time?"

Another vital aspect of an effective practice session is, quite simply, for me to be there, on the court, with the team the entire time. Some coaches will order a drill and then walk off. But I believe you have to do more than that if you expect to have the team get the job done. A leader has to work through the process with them so that he *knows* they will perform their jobs well during a game. You can't just tell people what to do and then expect them to perform well.

One of the great things about coaching is that each day is different—including practices. There was a time when my lesson plan was chiseled in stone. As a matter of fact, I went crazy if we got off schedule or a few minutes behind. But remembering to be flexible in what and how I teach is a lesson I've learned over the years. Now, I hope I'm a little wiser and a little more innovative. If I see something that needs to be addressed in practice, I don't hesitate to change the day's schedule. Rather than it being chiseled in stone, I use my plan as more of a guide.

A leader may be the most knowledgeable person in the world, but if the players on his team cannot translate that knowledge into action, it means nothing. In other words, it's not what *I know,* it's what *they do* on the court that really matters. And if we're playing hard in practice, under gamelike conditions, then we're just naturally going to play smarter and better during a game. That's why all our practice drills are as gamelike as possible.

We put make-believe scores in practice. We work on end-of-half situations, end-of-game situations, foul situations, and timeouts. That's right! We'll actually practice a timeout. During a break, while the guys are drinking their water, I'll set up a situation or bring home a lesson point—and then they're right back on the court. We'll also practice shooting free throws in the middle of the practice when the players are out of breath—just like they'll be out of breath during a game. Also, I never use a whistle in practice. I want the players to get used to reacting to my voice—just like in a real game.

A whistle is like a crutch and I don't feel like I'm standing on my own two feet when I use one. Besides, a whistle puts some distance between me and the players. And I'm a big believer in cutting out anything that tends to add to that distance—especially if it's something as artificial as a whistle. That's one reason I don't rely very heavily on e-mail, phone messages, or memos. There's something impersonal about them. They don't tend to foster relationships among people. I'd rather sit down and talk.

My belief is that when we do enough little things in practice that simulate what will occur during a game, we'll put ourselves in a position to win every time. Having a chance to win each time out is one of my goals.

Seeing Themselves Through Your Eyes

I want all the players on our team to see themselves through my eyes. They need to know how they *really* are, not just how they *think* they are. If they can step outside themselves and watch their performances as I see them, then they may internalize both their shortcomings and their strengths.

That's why videotape is very important in my business. Because any way you cut it, when a player sees himself on videotape—as the coach sees him—you can bet your life, he's going to try to improve. And that helps not only individual performance, but overall team effectiveness.

Before a practice, I may call our team's head manager over and ask him to focus the video camera on one player for about fifteen minutes of practice. Actually, I'll tape all of the guys a time or two without telling them in advance. After we sit down with them and show them the video, they usually work harder in practice because they figure they'll be on tape and don't want to look bad or be embarrassed.

We make it a habit to view videotapes after practices and games because we want our players accustomed to dealing with the truth that the camera reveals. During a practice, I may tell Matt Christensen that he's not doing a good job of screening. But while he's saying, "Yes, sir," he might also be thinking, "What does he want from me today? I'm screening." However, when I sit down with him and we watch the tape together, he'll see it for himself. "Coach is right. I'm not screening." Matt Christensen will then become more responsible about his   91 actions. Not only that, he'll want to learn more. "How can I get better at screening?" he might ask.

On a more positive note, I might mention to Nate James during a game that he's doing a terrific job of rebounding. And afterward, when the team watches the videotape together, I'll point out Nate's exceptional work. People like to see themselves on tape doing great things—and they also feel good about a compliment, especially when it's in front of their peers.

For the players to see themselves through my eyes is not always a pleasant thing. But always, it is a fact. Always, it is the truth. Sometimes, however, the truth can be brutal—as it was when I sat down in a one-on-one videotape session with Bobby Hurley.

Bobby had the strongest look of anybody I ever coached. It was an indescribable look of confidence, of determination. And when he had that look, he'd make behind-the-back passes and long three-point shots. He just inspired everybody around him. Bobby's face was also a window to his heart. When he had his window dressed right, it made us all better. But if he reacted in a negative manner to anything, it changed not only the window, but it changed the heart of our entire team.

Well, in his first few years, Bobby had a habit of wearing his emotions on his sleeve. Once in a while, he appeared to be pouting on the court and his negative reaction to referee calls often became major distractions to his teammates.

So one day I had a five-minute videotape compiled of nothing but shots of Hurley's facial expressions during games. Then I sat him down in private and showed him how he looked to me and to everyone else on the court. He saw himself pouting, whining, pointing fingers, dropping his head, and losing his temper. When the tape finished, I leaned over to him and quietly said: "Bobby, is that the message you want to send to your teammates?"

I honestly don't think he realized just how much his development was being impeded by his emotional reactions. Even though it was painful to watch, Bobby Hurley responded by becoming one of the best point guards to ever play college basketball. And he went on to lead Duke to two national championships.

While I worked with Hurley privately, I chose a different approach with his teammate Christian Laettner.

Near the end of one season, Christian had a particularly awful performance in a game against North Carolina. So I had a three-minute tape made that highlighted only him. Then I called everybody into our locker room, closed the doors, and ran the tape.

After it was over, I looked my star player dead in the eye: "Your look, the yelling, your whole performance, was unacceptable. You were bad, Christian. And that bothers me because you're not bad, you're one hell of a basketball player. But if you do that again, you're not going to play. And if you don't believe me, test me. I will not allow us to beat ourselves."

Then, in front of all his teammates, Christian looked me in the eye and said: "Coach, it will never happen again."

And it didn't. We went on in postseason to win the NCAA tournament and Laettner was named college basketball Player of the Year.

Years after leaving Duke and going on to a successful career in the NBA, Christian Laettner told a reporter: "We won championships at Duke because of what happened behind closed doors."

Plan for Nuances

I teach many different concepts during the course of the regular season. But one thing I always attempt to do is prepare our team for as many little things, as many nuances as possible that they may encounter in a game situation. The reason I go to all the trouble is quite simply because other coaches may not do it. So it might provide us with an edge that could put us in a position to win the game.

A good example involves the concepts of individual and team fouls that occur during every basketball game. Each individual player is allowed five personal fouls before he's automatically out of the game. If a team, collectively, racks up seven fouls in a half, the opponent gets to go to the foul line for a one-and-one situation. Before that, they just get the ball out of bounds. Ten team fouls mean that the opposing team automatically gets to shoot two free throws. Now that's a pretty big penalty that can change the entire character of a game.

People often wonder why Duke shoots so many more free throws than our opponents. As a matter of fact, in most years, we *make* more free throws than our opponents *attempt.*

Many of those who wonder how we achieve such a one-sided statistic usually chalk it up to luck. "Well, Duke is lucky. They get all the breaks."

Baloney. Just like any smart business leader, we plan for it.

How does a great company win more contracts than their competition? They plan and practice for it. They look at all the subtle nuances of their business and they are ready when they go into competition. Right? Well, one of the nuances of my business revolves around fouls. It not only *happens* every game, it has a tremendous *bearing* on every game. So we plan for it.

Basically, I try to teach the team that all fouls are *our* fouls. "When *one* of us fouls," I'll tell the players, "*all* of us foul." Sometimes, when I'm running a game situation in practice, like a 20-minute scrimmage to simulate a half, I'll send in a substitute.

"Stop," I'll say to the sub just before he enters the game. "How many team fouls do we have?"

"Uh, don't know."

"Sit down!"

Then I'll either call up the next guy or I'll stop the action and turn the ball over to the other team.

"What's that for?" the guys on the court will complain.

"Jason didn't know how many team fouls we had."

That forces each guy sitting on the bench to think that it's his team out on the court. And it also keeps his head in the game while he's on the sidelines so he'll be better prepared once he gets in the game.

Some coaches have a hard rule that if any one of their players gets two fouls in the first half, he sits down for the rest of the half. Boy do I like that rule—not for my team, but for their team.

If I know ahead of time that an opposing coach has that rule, I might plan to attack that player with two quick fouls so he has to sit down. On the other hand, if one of our guys, say Trajan Langdon, gets two early fouls, instead of sitting him down for the rest of the half, I might pull him out for a minute and talk to him.

"Okay, Tray, here's the situation. You're going to play. In fact, you may play fourteen more minutes in this half. But you're not going to get another foul and you're going to play hard. You now have a chance to do something that most people could never do. Most guys would be conservative. But I want you to learn how to attack, how to play defense—and have the incredible discipline not to foul. Can you do that?"

"Yes."

"Okay, get back out there."

In general, we focus on all of the nuances of the game as both individual and collective responsibilities. Many business organizations do exactly the same thing. If one department is down, but another is doing okay, a good team doesn't allow comments like, "Well, everything is okay because my department is fine." No. If one of us is not doing well, all of us are not doing well.

This concept teaches camaraderie, confidence, discipline, collective thinking, and teamwork. Not only that, fouls are a nuance that happens in every single game. Therefore, it is a subtlety that is critical to address. By doing so, we are staying on top of performance. That's what any good business leader would do, say, for a salesperson. What can you do better the next time? What are the "fouls" in your business?

Creativity and Innovation

In basketball, positions are traditionally numbered, 1-2-3-4-5, for each player on the court. But I never use numbers to designate a position—never.

In addition, I shy away from even stating that certain players have to play certain positions. People could call Quin Snyder a point guard, for instance, but Billy King and Danny Ferry, his teammates, would still bring the ball up the court—which, according to the strict definition of the position, only a point guard should do.

It's similar to the reluctance I have of forcing somebody into a job description. If a coach tries to force a kid into a role he cannot handle, then there's a tendency to say that the kid is no good. But that same individual might be a heck of a player in a different position or in another role. I think it's more important to concentrate on the character and talent of the individual player rather than on the number, the position, or the job description.

Every year our team loses a player or two to graduation. And every year I'm asked, "How are you going to replace a Tommy Amaker, or a Johnny Dawkins, or a Danny Ferry?" Well, we don't replace guys like that. It's not possible. There will never be another Tommy Amaker or Johnny Dawkins or Danny Ferry. We don't even try to replace them. Why create the expectation that we can?

If I were to try every year to replace a previous player, or fill a predesignated slot, or tie a new person to a number, I would be doing a grave injustice not only to the individual, but to the team as a whole. Doing so puts limits on individual talent and artistry. And that's the last thing in the world I want for our team. I want no artificial walls erected that might limit potential, stifle creativity, or shackle innovation.

At Duke, nobody is a number. Rather, we try to plant seeds that help people grow. We try to give every individual the freedom to develop their full capabilities.

If you put a plant in a jar, it will take the shape of the jar. But if you allow the plant to grow freely, twenty jars might not be able to hold it. The freedom to grow personally, the freedom to make mistakes and learn from them, the freedom to work hard, and the freedom to be yourself—these four freedoms should be guaranteed by every leader in every organization.

There are a couple of other things I do to encourage creativity and innovation in all the teams I coach.

I try to mix things up, for example, to provide as much variety as I possibly can so that people don't fall into ruts or become bored. That's why at practice, I try to pick different places to talk to the team and try to dream up new drills and make them as gamelike as possible.

Leaders should be reliable without being predictable. They should be consistent without being anticipated. Instead of providing a spawning ground for creativity, a leader may be so structured, so ruled, so totally predictable, that he completely erases any enjoyment on the part of the team. I recall one year, for instance, when our guys had been playing very poorly and expected a good chewing out from me. But when they showed up for practice, they found a volleyball net set up on the court. And that's all we did during that practice—play volleyball. I felt the players had forgotten what it was like to have fun playing ball.

In any classroom, if the students can predict what the teacher is going to do all the time, they start memorizing and stop thinking. Too many rules and too much predictability absolutely kill creativity.

Another thing I like to do is ask questions—lots of questions. If a player is looking for an answer, for instance, rather than just telling him straight out, I may ask him a series of questions so that he'll think for himself and try to reason the answer out. That way, he'll remember the solution better and be more likely to implement it.

I learned this technique of asking questions from two great basketball coaches, Hank Iba and Pete Newell. I had the good fortune to be around them early in my career. And when I had the opportunity, I would frequently ask them how I could improve.

"Did you watch our game?" I'd ask Coach Iba or Coach Newell. "What do you think?"

Invariably, neither coach would give me a specific. Rather, the conversation would go something like this:

"Well, you know your team better than anybody. But have you looked at your offense on the help side? Have you looked to see what they're doing?"

Then I'd press for details. "What did you see?" I'd ask.

"Just take a look on the help side on offense. Look at it yourself."

So I would take a look myself and then I'd go back to the coach.

"We're not moving."

"Right."

"What should I do?"

"Well, what would *you* do?"

If I didn't give Coach Iba or Coach Newell the right answer, they'd ask me another question in an effort to lead me to the correct solution. But always, always they would make sure that I came up with the solution myself. They would not just tell me the answer.

And the fact is that I always remembered these solutions better. I would think about the situation myself, determine the right answer, and I would *never* forget it. I also noticed that I was more determined to implement my newfound solution in practice. And I was better able to teach it to my players.

Subsequently, I took this technique of asking questions to another level—one that really helps to enhance my own creativity and innovation. I'll frequently ask a variety of people how they see our team. What are our strengths and weaknesses? Do they see any problems? What do they think we need to work on?

I may ask my secretary, or our sports information director, or my wife questions like these. And I'll ask D.C., the person who cleans our locker room.

"Are they sloppier than usual, D.C.?"

"No, Coach, they're pretty good."

"Do you think any of the kids are having any personal problems?"

"Not that I can tell."

"Will you keep an eye on them for me, D.C.?"

"Sure will, Coach."

Well, there have been a couple of times when I've been working in the locker room on something and D.C., who's been cleaning in the background, will pipe up with a comment.

"Hey, Coach, I think Nate might have gotten a bad grade on a test. Doesn't seem to be himself right now."

"Thanks, D.C. I'll keep an eye on him in practice tomorrow."

I wouldn't have known about that potential problem unless I had already opened up a line of communication with D.C. Leaders aren't the only people who can think of innovative things. Good ideas can come from anywhere and everywhere. And often, they may come from the people you least expect to have them.

My mom was a cleaning woman. She was also the best person I've ever known. And she had all kinds of great ideas. So I figure that anybody in any job can have a good idea.

Can the person who cleans the floor in your organization give you a suggestion? And more importantly, will you listen to that person?

Coach K's Tips

- When teaching, always remember this simple phrase: "You hear, you forget. You see, you remember. You do, you understand."

- Go in fully prepared for every practice. Create a lesson plan. But stay flexible. Use it only as a guide.

- A leader cannot just tell people what to do and then expect them to perform well.

- Cut out anything that tends to put distance between you and members of your team.

- Members of your team need to see themselves through your eyes—so that they may see how they *really* are, not how they *think* they are.

- Plan for as many nuances as you can. Address the little things you may encounter in a real situation.

- Erect no artificial walls that might limit potential, stifle creativity, or shackle innovation.

- Leaders should be reliable without being predictable. They should be consistent without being anticipated.

- Ask questions—lots of questions.

- Good ideas can come from anywhere and everywhere.

7

TURN NEGATIVES INTO POSITIVES

"Sometimes adversity can work in your favor. Instead of feeling sorry for yourself and using it as an excuse, accept the situation and try to make the most of it. That's how a team develops resilience and character."

—Coach K

"A little negative thing must be dealt with immediately—before it becomes a big negative thing."

—Coach K

"Don't worry about losing. Think about winning."

—Coach K

*T*here are seven minutes left in the first half. Clemson is ahead by two points. It's been a close game to this point. We have not been able to capture the momentum even though we're at home.

Clemson is playing hard, inspired basketball each and every time they come down the court. We need to break their momentum with all-out, tough defense. It's their ball out of bounds. Here they come again. Let's go.

As the action resumes, Trajan Langdon and Shane Battier play particularly close to their men. They are really working hard to prevent the visitors from getting off a good shot. Things are looking good until, all of a sudden, Trajan takes an elbow to the mouth and drops face-first to the floor. He doesn't get up. He just lies there—bleeding profusely.

It's February 20, 1999, and our star senior, our leading

scorer, is lying on the court bleeding from the mouth. This is not a practice simulation. This is a real game.

From my vantage point on the Duke bench, it appeared that Langdon had been flagrantly coldcocked by the Clemson player—and I was livid. I immediately rushed over to Trajan and motioned for our trainer. When I saw that my player's upper lip had been split in two, I looked over at the Clemson coach and angrily jerked my right elbow to the side, demonstrating what I just saw. "That was flagrant!" I yelled.

After a few minutes, the bleeding was stabilized and we helped Trajan to his feet. I don't recall who helped him off the court, but I suddenly realized I had to switch from the role of concerned parent to that of tough leader.

As I stormed back to my place on the bench, I tore off my suit coat and threw it under the scorer's table. I didn't do it to make a point to my players, although I'm sure they noticed it. I was just angry and it was time to get to work. We needed to react as a team. We could not go back out on the court as if nothing had happened.

When I got back to the huddle, the first thing I said to the players was that I had seen what happened. "Looked flagrant to me," I said.

Then I grabbed Elton Brand and Shane Battier by the jerseys: "I want you to go after them," I said. "I want all of you guys to get more physical. We're not going to take this off of anybody. We're not going to let them do that to Trajan—or to anybody else on our team. Got it?"

At that point, I could see the fire in their eyes—and I realized I didn't have to say anything else. Shane Battier was particularly intense. I distinctly remember him yelling, "Let's go, let's go, let's go," to his teammates as they went back into action. And our players knew that I was not telling them to go 105 back out there and start a brawl. They knew what I wanted them to do—and they did it.

Over the next six minutes, we went on a 26–0 scoring run. And the game was over at halftime.

Pay Attention to Detail

Some teams might have panicked in a situation like that. After all, we were having a tough time with Clemson up until that point. And then to have our leader on the court, our leading scorer, taken out due to an injury, could have served to be a real downer or, worse yet, an excuse to give up.

Our team turned that negative situation into a victory largely because I led them in that direction. That's my job. I'm the head coach.

But to tell you the truth, I don't believe it ever would have happened if I had not noticed in that split second that Trajan had been smashed in the face. If I had not been intensely focused on every facet of what was happening on the court, I would not have taken my coat off and thrown it. I would not have been angry. And I would not have led our team to the emotional fever pitch they eventually reached.

I have always had a bit of a gift for noticing virtually everything that happens on the court during a game. Of course, my attention to detail focuses on all the technical aspects of the game—whether a player is rotating well on defense, whether another is following through on his jump shot, whether we're balanced on offense, and so on. But while it's important for a leader to focus on the technical details of his industry or business, I also believe it's *vital* to focus on details related specifically to people in the organization.

People talk to you in different ways—through facial expressions, moods, mannerisms, body language, the tone in their voice, the look in their eyes. As a coach, I must be able to read my players, to recognize those different things and then take appropriate action.

This aspect of leadership is fascinating to me. To figure out what the members of my team are thinking, to determine who they are at one particular moment in time, is not only a necessity for a leader, it's a great challenge. Sometimes, I may be wrong in my interpretation, but if I have built strong relationships and spent quite a bit of time observing and listening, I'll usually be pretty close to the truth.

When Bobby Hurley had that look on his face, I didn't have to say anything to him. But when he did not have that look, I knew it was time for me to do something. I had to work on him mentally and get him in a positive frame of mind. And that might mean challenging him, chastising him, or simply putting my arm around him and giving him a smile.

I became effective at working with Bobby, as I do all of my players, by practicing reads. I make it a point not to go into a game without taking a look each day at the members of our team to see how they're doing and what they might be thinking.

How a kid walks out on the court during practice, for example, might be a tip-off. Usually, he's talking a little bit to one of his buddies. But maybe this time he's keeping a little bit more to himself.

So, I'll walk up to him and ask, "What's up?"

"Just flunked a big test."

"Well, I know how bad you feel. It'll be all right. Let's have a good practice now and we'll talk about it afterward."

Situations like this one happen daily and every leader 107

must be alert to deal with them as they occur. Any little negative thing can hurt the team's overall performance. So it must be dealt with immediately before it becomes a big negative thing.

Think About Winning

Both good and bad events will take place as the season progresses. When the bad stuff happens, I'm always looking for a way to turn it into something that will work for us. I believe a leader has to be positive about all the things that happen to his team. How can you turn unsuccessful things into successful things?

Overcoming adversity is part of becoming successful. And dealing with losses, mistakes, and bad breaks is simply part of life.

The Clemson game in 1999 was a good example of turning a negative into a positive. But in that circumstance, we lost Trajan Langdon for only a short time. As a matter of fact, after getting seven stitches in his lip, Trajan came back and played in the second half, which, of course, gave our team another tremendous burst of emotion.

On the last day of January 1992, however, something much more serious happened to the Duke basketball team— Bobby Hurley broke his foot and we lost him for three and a half weeks. Our team was really cruising along at that point and I really felt we were the best team in the country. But when Hurley went down, I could tell that the other players were worried.

There was no time to mope, however. We had to deal with this situation and we had to deal with it fast because we had to play a particularly tough contest against Louisiana State University down in Baton Rouge.

The year before, we had beaten LSU—whose star player was Shaquille O'Neal. But he was only a freshman then and we had played them at home in Cameron Indoor Stadium. O'Neal, who was arguably the most talked-about player in the NCAA that year, had been eyeing the rematch. In fact, I recall reading in the paper that he had "circled that date on my calendar." "I'm going to beat Laettner," he also said. "We're going to kill Duke."

When we arrived in Louisiana, we found that LSU had pulled out all the stops for us. They had their live tiger on the court. It was the first time students had camped out overnight to get into a basketball game and the place was packed. Actually, LSU was like a war zone. Outside the arena, when our guys got off the bus, some students poured drinks and beer on us. Inside, we were sneered at and booed unbelievably.

I believe most kids would have been intimidated by such a brawling demonstration. But I swear Christian Laettner loved it. And when the rest of the team saw him energized rather than terrified, it gave them courage to fight. No one was saying, "Woe is me," or "These people are yelling at us," or "They have Shaquille O'Neal and he's out to kill us." There was no whining at all. And when they went out on the court, they played one hell of a game.

Of course, we had to adjust our system a bit with Bobby out. It was the first time Grant Hill played at the point guard position and we also changed our attack on LSU's zone defense. But the big difference in the game was Laettner—who played like a man possessed. When we brought him up from the baseline, he hit the three-point shots. When he was down

109

under, he fought O'Neal successfully for big rebounds. He just did everything right.

We needed Laettner's heart to win that game. And he came through. But Christian is the type of player who will drive a dagger into your heart in the midst of heated competition.

With less than a minute left and the game well in hand, Laettner was fouled. And as he ran down the court to the foul line, he started giving it back to the fans—taunting them by holding his index finger in the air and indicating that "We're number one, not LSU." At that point, I called a timeout.

"Christian," I said to him in the huddle, "do you like life?"

"Yeah, Coach."

"Well, don't do that. We've won the game. Let's get out of here alive, okay?"

Then I told the rest of the team to cool it. "When the buzzer sounds," I said, "don't be running up and down. Don't be jumping around. Walk off the court like you knew you were going to win here. Instead of high-fiving, let's walk out with class."

And that's exactly what we did. We walked off the court quietly and with an air of confidence—like we played our normal game. Just a routine game. That's what we do. Why should we celebrate? And several people looking on in the stands and at home on television later mentioned to me that, at that moment, "Duke looked like they expected to win all along." And that's what we wanted all of our future opponents to believe— that even without Bobby Hurley, *we expected to win.*

Of course, in the privacy of our own locker room and on the bus back home, there was whooping and hollering and celebrating. We all knew that we had played a great, great ball game. And it was one that the entire 1992 team would look back on as one of the best experiences of the season.

On that day, we met adversity and turned a negative into a positive. Instead of feeling sorry for ourselves and using Hurley's injury as an excuse, we accepted the situation and made the most of it.

The U.S. Military Academy taught me a very key principle: "Don't worry about losing. Think about winning." In other words, even when you have a loss, you must ask yourself, "What is good about this? How can I turn a defeat into something that works for us?"

I don't look at anything in the past as failure. I look at it as a great experience. Mistakes are part of the building process. Mistakes have to be made. How you act when you make mistakes is of paramount importance. That's how both teams and individuals grow and improve.

But the truth is that most business teams lose that game at LSU. They lose it even before the whistle sounds to start play. They have built-in excuses to lose, rationalizations as to why they didn't have a chance. "We lost our key salesman. The people were hostile toward us. We couldn't have won that contract. We did as well as we could have done under the circumstances."

Forget it!

They could have walked out of there with a win!

Remember, sometimes adversity can work in your favor. Instead of feeling sorry for yourself and using it as an excuse, accept the situation and try to make the most of it. That's how a team develops resilience and character.

The Courage to Lead

Now, of course, we don't win every game. But we can learn from every game. We also have to make important decisions during every game. And it takes courage not only to make the tough decisions, but to live with those decisions after they're made—whether we end up with a win or a loss.

In our 1999 national championship loss to the University of Connecticut, I had a particularly tough decision to make during the final minute of play. Entering the game, we were 37-1. We were ranked number one in the polls and seeded number one in the East. And we were heavily favored to win the championship.

It was a close game all the way, but during the later stages, UConn began to pull away somewhat. And if it were not for Trajan Langdon, we would have lost by 10 points. But Duke was riding Langdon's heart that day. In the last five minutes, UConn would make a great play, then Langdon would make a great play. UConn made a play. Langdon made a play.

Then came the final minute and, even though we were one point down, I felt we had seized the momentum of the game. From the bench, I decided to signal for a set play where Trajan would bring the ball up the court, read the defense, and then react based on what he saw. He could pass the ball to Chris Carrawell, hit Elton Brand in the low post, or take a shot himself. Unfortunately, he was called for traveling and we ended up losing the national championship.

The way I look at it is simple: UConn was better than we were at that particular point in the game—and on that particular day. The truth is that we were beaten by a very good basketball team.

After the game, people criticized me for not calling a timeout. Well, if I thought my team was in disarray, I would have called one. But, at that point, they looked confident and I decided to let them go. Besides, we had practiced many times the play we were going with. Actually, as far as I was concerned, no other play would have worked that day. We had to follow Langdon's heart because nobody else had stepped up to take the lead. It was the winning thing to do at that moment in that particular situation—even though we did not win the game.

Now, if we had made a basket on that play and we had won the ball game, rather than criticizing, people might have said: "What a brilliant move! He had the *courage* not to call a timeout! He *trusted* his team. He went to something they've practiced in gamelike situations and it worked."

If we had won, that's what would have been said. But, as we lost, it was: "You should've called a timeout. Why did you go to Langdon? What the hell were you thinking?"

Well, that's the world I live in, so I have to be prepared for it.

Actually, I'm good with whichever way it goes if I follow my heart. I have to be. A leader has to have the courage to make a key decision in a split second. And then he has to have the courage to live with it afterward—whether it succeeds or fails. Because if he doesn't, he'll be afraid to make the next key decision. Courage and confidence are what decision-making is all about.

The day after the game, Mickie and I were at home in Durham watching the UConn team return home to thousands of cheering fans. When head coach Jim Calhoun stepped up to the microphone, all the television cameras were focused on him.

He was very eloquent with his words. He gave credit to the many UConn fans who had supported their team when they lost in the NCAA tournament the previous year.

"You met us here last year," he began, "and you helped us mend a broken heart. This was supposed to be the year of the Blue Devils."

Then Coach Calhoun made a comment that caused me to shake my head "no, no, no."

"Yesterday," he continued, "we kicked some butt and broke some hearts."

"No way," I said. "Losing a basketball game could never break my heart."

Coach K's Tips

- It's important for a leader to focus on the technical details of his industry or business. But it's *vital* to focus on details related specifically to people in the organization.

- People talk to you in different ways—through facial expressions, moods, mannerisms, body language, the tone in their voice, the look in their eyes.

- As a leader, you must be able to read your players.

- A leader has to be positive about all things that happen to his team. Look at nothing in the past as failure.

- You cannot win every game. But you can learn from every game.

- It takes courage not only to make decisions, but to live with those decisions afterward.

- A leader has to have the courage to make a key decision in a split second.

- Courage and confidence are what decision-making is all about.

- Don't let a single game break your heart.

8

GAME
DAY

"Every minute of the game, every moment that leads up to the game, I'm trying to think and plan and prepare myself and our players for anything that might happen—and that means putting some of my own emotions aside if they won't help us reach our goals."

—Coach K

"The train's moving fast right now, guys. Are you on board?"

—Coach K

"I coach by feel. I follow my heart."

—Coach K

The telephone rings in our house at 1:00 in the afternoon and Mickie picks up the receiver and answers.

"Hello."

"Hi, Mom," says our daughter Debbie. "Just wanted to check up on Dad. How's he doing?"

"The 'F' word," Mickie responds with a wry grin.

Mickie, my daughters, and my friends all know not to disturb me on the day we have a game. That's why they joke about the "F" word. "F" stands for "Focused." "Coach K has blinders on today. He sees nothing but what's in front of him—the game."

Debbie laughs on the other end of the line. "He's not too worried about the game tonight, is he?" she asks.

"He's fine, Debbie. Just going down for his nap. Typical game day stuff."

"Okay, well, tell him I'll be there tonight."

"I will. Love you. Bye."

*   *   *

Game day is the best of all days and it is sacred for me.

I try to be away from people as much as possible. I avoid all outside distractions. I take a nap. I relax. And I think about nothing but the upcoming game—our opponents, our players, my pregame remarks, our game strategy, all the possible game scenarios, and all the potential adjustments that will have to be made.

I want game day to be my best day. I take a nap so that I can clear my head of all distractions—so that I can be the best I can be for our team. They depend on me. They expect me to be in top form—upbeat, positive, confident, certain we can win—which is exactly what I expect from them.

My complete focus this particular day is precipitated by my total and absolute respect for our players and coaches, our university, our fans, and for the game itself. How does a person show respect for anything? He gives it time. If you respect your children, you give them time. If you respect your employees, you listen to them. You give them time. So, by taking that entire day and focusing on nothing but the game, I am showing respect for my profession and for the people who depend on me. It's part of my mutual commitment with them. I'm committed to giving them 100 percent and they're committed to me for the same.

I'm going to live up to my end of the bargain by being structured on game day—even though I'm not usually a very structured person. One of the reasons I take a nap is because my best thinking time occurs after a good night's sleep. That's when I'm most imaginative during the day. So, in order to capture that ability to think and be creative, I try to catch a few winks. That way, I'll be more likely to react well to whatever unpredictable situation occurs during the game.

I also encourage and expect that all our players will show up to the game well rested and ready to play. And for the most part, our teams have done that. It's one of the reasons we win on a consistent basis. I'm always reminding them to come to every game focused. "If you guys can get yourselves to a high level as individuals," I tell them, "then I can take you to a higher level as a team. But if you show up at a lower level, I'll have to spend most of my time getting you up to a level you should already have been at."

A Game of Adjustments

Basketball is organized chaos. You can be on offense, then defense—then back on offense, then defense again—all within a ten-second span of time.

After a player shoots the ball, for example, he is instantly on defense. If he makes the shot, the other team gets the ball out of bounds. If he misses, odds are the other team will get the rebound. Well, if he's successful on defense by stealing the ball, he's back on offense again. And then, if he shoots, he's right back on defense. All in ten seconds.

Like business, basketball almost never stands still. It stops only on the whistle—and then only for a few minutes at most. Moreover, anything can happen—and it often does. A coach can come in with a great plan and find that he has to throw it out after the first five minutes of competition.

"I thought our full-court press would work. It's not working. Got to adjust."

"I thought something we saw on videotape and tried to take advantage of would be good. It wasn't. Have to do something different."

"That guy's just hit two in a row. Got to get on him."

"Damn, I didn't know they were going to play a 1-2-2 defense. What do we do now?"

"Trajan Langdon just got his mouth busted open. Oh, no!"

And on, and on, and on.

That's the way it goes *every single game*.

It's like driving through midtown Manhattan. You know you're going to encounter a traffic jam in Times Square. But you don't know how long it will last, whether you'll encounter extra buses and trucks along with the cars, whether or not they'll be working on the streets, or whether there might be some construction. And you won't be able to see everything once you're in the middle of it. That's what a basketball game is like.

Therefore, basketball is a game of adjustments—just like business.

Adjustments are not *unusual,* they are *usual.* So a leader's ability to think on his feet—to react accordingly, to do things without instruction, to react to voices on the court, and to think outside of himself—is of paramount importance. That's one reason I focus and rest before every game. If I have a clearer head, I'm more apt to make better decisions while on the run. I'll be better able to adjust. Every minute of the game, every moment that leads up to the game, I'm trying to think and plan and prepare myself and our players for anything that might happen—and that means putting some of my own emotions aside if they won't help us reach our goals.

I recall a thrilling game Duke played against UConn in 1990.

With 2.6 seconds left in overtime and us down 78–77, we got the ball and I immediately called a timeout. In the huddle, I diagrammed a play and had everybody focused on executing

121

it properly. But as our players walked out on the court, I immediately noticed an opening in the defense that I had not counted on.

Rather than calling another timeout, I caught Christian Laettner's attention and called "special"—a play designed to take advantage of the opening. Brian Davis was watching me because he had a habit of always looking my way when we were in a tight situation.

Christian, who was inbounding the ball, mouthed the words, "Run special, Brian." So Davis took the inbounds pass and then quickly flipped the ball back to Laettner, who took a seventeen-foot shot, made it, and Duke won the basketball game.

The only three people who knew we were going to run that play were Laettner, Davis, and me. The other guys on our team were running the play I had previously called in the huddle—the one that probably wouldn't have worked. And they were as surprised as the UConn players at what happened.

Coach by Feel

Each game is a melting pot of all that happens each season.

There are thousands of people in the stands. We might be on the road. People might be yelling at us. Television cameras try to get into our huddles. There are bands playing, cheerleaders on the court. There's the emotion of the crowd, the emotion of the players, the emotion of the game itself.

There is also nervous anticipation. How are we going to do? All that stuff we talked about: face-to-face communication, eye-to-eye contact, the fist. All the gamelike situations. All the drills. Can the players hear my voice or do I have to start blow-ing a whistle? Are they really listening to me?

It's all being tested right now—on game day. Let's see how well we can talk. Let's see how hard we can play. Let's see how many loose balls we can get. Let's see. Let's see.

By the time we're ready to play a game, I hope I have fig-ured out what I'm going to say to the group in the locker room. Sometimes, because of something I see in their faces, I may have to say a little more than I've prepared. Other times, I might see by the look in their eyes that they are ready to play *right now*. So even if I've worked hard to prepare a five-minute pregame speech, rather than giving it only to hear myself talk, I'm going to adjust and not give the speech because I can see it would not help the team. In fact, it might even hurt them. Either way, I could not know whether to cut short or expand my remarks if I had not been previously practicing reads on each of my players' faces.

When the referee blows his whistle, all of a sudden the chaos begins and we're in the line of fire. Now what am I going to do? How will I handle each situation? How will I adjust?

When the players come over for a timeout, I might have two minutes. Do I talk that entire time? Sometimes, if the team is in trouble, I do.

What mood do I want to portray during that timeout? Are they down and playing lousy? Do I need to chastise them? "You guys stink right now! Get your drink of water! Towel off—*if* you're *sweating!* You may not need those towels right now."

Are they up and playing well? Maybe I should say nothing. "You guys are playing great! Just have a drink of water."

Is it an end-of-half or end-of-game situation? What type of situation is it?

What about during a 20-second timeout? Only 20 seconds to get a message across? You've got to be kidding!

There was a game at Georgia Tech in 1999. We were terrible. In fact, the guys didn't show up ready to play. With 38 seconds left in the first half, I called a timeout. I stepped into the huddle, looked at the players, then pulled back and sat down on the bench without saying a word. I also looked away. At that moment, I decided to coach by not coaching. And I believe they all got the message.

In the locker room at halftime, I looked at my watch and wrote "2:15–3:00" on the chalkboard. Then I wrote "45 minutes" in large letters and circled it.

"All right, listen up, fellas," I said. "Time is going to run out. In forty-five minutes you're going to be dead. You're going to heaven or hell. Where do you want to be?" We came back to win that game by a score of 87–79.

There was another, even more crucial game at Wake Forest in 1997 that I remember vividly. I felt we had to win that game. We were ranked eighth in the nation but were not playing as well as we could in the last few weeks—and we had lost nine straight games to Wake Forest and their senior star, Tim Duncan. As the team's leader, I viewed this game as an opportunity for our team to get to another level. It had the potential to be a defining moment.

So in the locker room before the game, I instinctively picked up a Magic Marker and drew a line on the floor. "Fellas," I said, "there comes a time when you take a stand and say, 'In order to cross this line, you're going to have to kill me.' We're winning right now. This is my country, it's my building, it's my ball! You're not getting this! This is ours!"

A lot of people never draw a line in the sand. We drew a line that day and it kept our season from going south. We won the game and went on to capture the ACC regular season title—something we achieved six times in the 1990s.

Game day is not a day for long, drawn-out speeches. It's a time for interaction. And you have to interact by feel.

That's what I do. I coach by feel. I follow my heart. And if I do it well enough and frequently enough with my team, my heart will come back to me a thousand times over in a thousand different ways.

During the 1985–1986 season, we were playing in the preseason NIT (National Invitation Tournament) before a capacity crowd in Madison Square Garden. Our opponent was St. John's University, who had two great stars in Mark Jackson and Walter Berry.

With 19 seconds left and Duke leading 71–70, St. John's got the ball and called a timeout. Walter Berry had scored 35 points—half his team's total. As our team walked over to the bench, I was thinking, "Walter Berry has scored 35 points, half his team's total. They're going to have him take the last shot. We haven't had anybody who's guarded him right this entire game. What am I going to do?"

But before I could say a word, David Henderson, our team co-captain, said: "Coach, let me guard Berry. I want him."

Now, David was a guard and Walter Berry played inside, which is usually considered a mismatch in Berry's favor. But I trusted Henderson and when I looked into his eyes, I saw the fire. So, instead of trying to plot out a more elaborate strategy, I followed my instinct.

"Okay, David," I said. "I trust you. He's yours."

When play resumed, St. John's tried to get the ball to Berry, but Henderson was all over him. So Mark Jackson was forced to shoot from the outside. His jump shot was short off the rim, David Henderson got the rebound, the buzzer sounded, and we won the game.

And I'll never forget David's reaction. He just pounded the ball to the floor and it bounced up into the air about twenty feet.

Two nights later, we beat Kansas, 92–86, and won the tournament.

All Aboard the Train

I speak often to our team about being on a train.

And the guys make jokes about it. "Has he talked about the damned train yet?"

I know they make jokes about it and I can see the smiles they crack and the looks they give one another when I mention it. But I talk about it anyway.

The train is the vehicle we are on for the journey. On board the train are all of our players, coaches, managers, staff—and all of the qualities we teach and believe in: the truth, the repetition in practice, the heart, the fist, everything.

During a critical period of the season, I might say something like: "The train's moving fast right now, guys. Are you on board?" Or I might tell them, "You can't be on someone else's train right now. You have to be on our train. We're moving and we're not stopping for you. Are you on it or not?"

I speak about the Duke basketball train at practices and at games. And the train stops at all games. As a matter of fact, each game is an intermediate stop on our journey. We get off the train and see how we're doing. Games are not our final destination. They are checkpoints on our progress—and we all realize that once the game is over, win or lose, it becomes part of the season.

Sometimes wonderful things happen on those intermediate stops. It might be the day we experience a great shot or a great comeback. Or more importantly, it might be the night one of our kids becomes a man. Let me give you a couple of examples.

Christian Laettner was emotionally spent in our 1992 national championship game with the University of Michigan. He had been our battering ram all year, our rock. But the first half of this game was the worst of Christian's career. He passed the ball more to Michigan than he did to Duke. In fact, he had more turnovers (seven) than he did points (five) in the first half.

I tried all sorts of different things to get him to snap out of it.

I subbed for him three different times. The first time, I said, "Come on, man, you're okay." The second time, I asked, "What's wrong? Let's get going." The third time, "You're not going to let us down *now,* are you?"

Nothing I said seemed to have an impact on him. But something unusual finally got to Laettner. In the locker room at halftime, Bobby Hurley—the usually quiet, reserved, do-your-talking-on-the-court Bobby Hurley—ripped into Christian Laettner and gave him a royal chewing out. He had never done that before. And everybody listened—especially Laettner.

Well, Christian came out in the second half and played much better. He was still tired, but he willed the performance out of himself. With just under seven minutes left, I sensed a breaking point in the game. So I called time when we had the ball and a three-point lead.

In the huddle, I began to diagram a play and looked first at Grant Hill.

"Grant, you take the ball . . ."

Then I stopped and turned to Laettner.

"No, wait," I said. "Christian, do you feel it?"

"Yes."

"Okay, Laett, you take the ball out of bounds. When you get it back, I want you to take a three-point shot. They're not going to play you out there. Take the three and hit it. We're going to win this game right now."

Well, Laettner got the ball back, fumbled it, and then got it back again. By this time, he was inside the three-point line. But he had committed himself to scoring, so he moved toward the basket and made the most god-awful move in the history of NCAA tournament play. Three Michigan players attempted to block his shot—but somehow, some way, the ball went in the basket. On the very next play, he stole the ball and fed Grant Hill for a driving layup. We outscored Michigan 23–6 to win going away, 71–51. And to this day, I still believe that it was Bobby Hurley's outburst in the locker room at halftime that won that game for us.

Grant Hill was a sophomore in that locker room. And two years later, in 1994, he was a senior when we played in the Southeast Regional championship game in Knoxville, Tennessee. Laettner and Hurley were gone—they were in the NBA. Our opponent was Purdue University with their talented star, Glen "Big Dog" Robinson, the nation's leading scorer. They were a really good team led by a great player—and coached by Gene Keady, one of the best. The game received a lot of press, in part, because Duke and Purdue were the top two seeds in the region.

During the first half, one of our freshmen, Jeff Capel, was playing particularly well—and I sensed that his matchup was going to be a key for us in the second half. So in the locker room at halftime, when I spoke to the team, I singled out Capel.

"You're the guy in the second half, Jeff," I said. "You're playing a great game. You're better than that guy. But you can really dominate him if you try. That's one of the things we can do in the second half. Okay?"

"Okay."

As I walked into the other room to talk to our assistant coaches for a moment, I heard Grant Hill pipe up in the background.

"That's right, Jeff. Coach is right. You can beat that guy. You can be great today."

Here was our team's star player, a senior encouraging a freshman on the team, during a crucial moment. As a coach, I was delighted because Hill saying that to Jeff Capel was much better than me saying it alone. It was another voice.

We came out in the second half and Capel scored the first five points to give us a 46–41 lead. But with 10 minutes to go in the game and Duke ahead by eight points, Grant picked up his fourth foul. And I distinctly remember looking skyward and thinking to myself: "God, thank you. It's been a great run." I knew it was impossible to win this game with Grant on the bench. We just weren't a strong-enough team without him. And besides, Purdue would now be much more confident with Hill out of the lineup.

Of course, I did not let the team know what I was thinking. And I also did everything I could to help us win the game. 129

I put Grant on the bench with four fouls and began thinking about when to bring him back in. And before going back onto the court, I noticed that Jeff Capel pulled the team together for a quick huddle. "Okay, guys," he said, "Grant carried us this far. It's time for us to step up."

Our team then rose to the occasion and played some of the greatest team basketball I have ever witnessed. By the time I put Grant back in, with about three minutes left to go, our team was well on their way to a thrilling victory. Chris Collins, Tony Lang, Cherokee Parks, and our sixth man, Marty Clark, all played as well as I had ever seen them play. But it was Jeff Capel who had the largest presence during those few minutes. He had a monster game—finishing with 19 points, four rebounds, and seven assists.

That game was one of those magic moments when everything I had taught them as a team came together. It did not depend on one guy. It did not depend on one voice. It depended on all of us. And we were the best that we could be.

After the game was over—after we had finished cutting down the nets with the realization that we were going to the Final Four—Grant Hill came up to me and apologized.

"Coach, I'm sorry," he said.

I put my arm around him as we were walking off the court, smiled, and said, "Grant, you won the game for us."

And he gave me this funny look. "No way," he replied. "I almost screwed it up with all those fouls."

"No, son, you won the game at halftime. You won it when you told Jeff Capel that he could be great today. And he was. In fact, he was the difference in the game when you were out. He lifted everybody else up to a higher level. You won the game for us just as sure as if you had been on the court the entire time. I'm proud of you."

Grant looked at me and nodded. He knew I was right.

When we got into the locker room, just as I do after every contest, I said a few words and we had our team prayer. Then later, as always, I called my mom to talk about the game.

COACH K'S TIPS

- Make game day your best day.
- The people on your team expect you to be upbeat, positive, confident, and certain they can win.
- Leaders show respect for people by giving them time.
- Make sure you have a clear head when you go into a game. That way, you'll be more likely to react well to whatever unpredictable situation might occur.
- Encourage every member of your team to be well rested and at a high level emotionally before every contest.
- Business, like basketball, is a game of adjustments. So be ready to adjust.
- You might have to throw out your well-crafted plan after only five minutes.
- You may have to put some of your own emotions aside if you are to help your team reach its goals.
- Sometimes a leader has to draw a line in the sand.
- Game day is not a day for long, drawn-out speeches. It is a time for interaction.
- Make sure everybody's on board the train.

POSTSEASON

REFRESH AND RENEW
- March Madness
- We're 0-0
- Media and Public Relations
- Believe but Don't Assume

FOCUS ON THE TASK AT HAND
- The Final Four
- Winning the Moment
- Handling Success
- Next Game

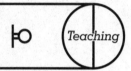

Commitment

Teaching

Family

Motivation

Excellence

HANDLING A CRISIS
- Truth and Trusting Relationships
- Have Fun
- Show the Face Your Team Needs to See
- Trying to Get to Heaven

CELEBRATE TRADITION
- A Part of Something Bigger
- Binding the Past to the Present
- The Sixth Man

"Like the springtime, our team is beginning anew. This is the time of the year when we not only must be playing our best basketball, but when we should be our most enthusiastic about playing."

—COACH K

9

REFRESH AND RENEW

"One of *the* worst things anybody can do is assume. I think fools assume. If people have *really* got it together, they never assume anything. They believe, they work hard, and they prepare—but they don't assume."

—Coach K

"Everybody doesn't just come together right away, meet on a mountaintop, and embrace. That's not the way it happens."

—Coach K

"Fellas, we're zero and zero—no wins and no losses."

—Coach K

I love the springtime.

Spring breathes new life into the world as trees start to bud and flowers begin to bloom. And it also breathes new life into me, personally. It gets me going, gets me refreshed and renewed, energized and excited.

It's a good thing, too, because I really need an adrenaline push at this time of the year. You see, while spring is refreshing and renewing, it can also be distracting and chaotic. That's because with the springtime comes madness—March Madness, the NCAA tournament.

For some teams, the season is over after the regular season. But for us, a well-planned, strategic rebirth is the order of the day. I think this principle is one of the reasons I have such a high winning percentage in postseason play. We really focus intensely on renewing everything. So I talk to the team about being excited, reenergizing themselves, and beginning anew.

When March rolls around, our family likes to use the expression, "We can see the beach." But we're not at the beach yet. We can't take our vacation yet. And we don't want the players to be in that frame of mind, either.

We've got a tournament to compete in.

March Madness

National media attention is astronomical during the postseason. And the hype begins immediately with the national television broadcast of the tournament selections and pairing brackets. Who should be there? Who shouldn't? Who are the favorites? Who are the underdogs? Who might be the Cinderella stories?

Every newspaper in the United States carries the brackets. Everybody's talking about the tournament. Everybody's a fan. Even people who weren't fans during the regular season are following the tournament—because now they have a chance to fill in all those blanks for an entire month.

And people love to fill in blanks. Husbands and wives compare selections. "Who did you take in the East Regional?" "I took Purdue." "No, no, I think Temple is going to win it all."

Millions of people participate in office pools. Almost everybody can make a connection in some way—their alma mater, their city, the state in which they live. Someone who lives in Detroit will call up a relative in Los Angeles. "I told you Gonzaga was going to beat UCLA!"

It gives people something to talk about. Even my own family becomes consumed with the tournament. They look at the brackets. My brother calls my wife. My daughter calls my sister-in-law. "Duke's in the East. If we make it to the Sweet Sixteen, we might meet Cincinnati—the only team that beat us this year. Boy would I like another crack at them!"

There's nothing else like the brackets of the NCAA tournament. There really isn't.

And there's no better time of the year. Because now our team is going to be ultimately tested. This is what we played the regular season for. But it's different than the regular season, in part, because your every move is magnified. And, now, if we lose, we're done. There will be no more games, no more tomorrows.

So how do we handle it all? How do we get the kids to focus on the job at hand when there's a big party going on and everyone's excited? How do we prepare the team for the tournament—for the craziness, the chaos, and the pandemonium of March Madness? How do we continue to win?

We're 0-0

After our team has watched the pairings broadcast together, I'll usually call a meeting the very next morning to set the tone for the upcoming tournament.

"Fellas, we're zero and zero—no wins and no losses," I'll say as I write 0-0 on the board. "Everybody in this tournament is zero and zero. And you know what? If we're fortunate to advance, after each game, we'll be zero and zero again. All season long, we've assumed that there is going to be another game. We play, get ready for another game, play and get ready for another game. Well, we can't assume anything anymore. There's a finality to the NCAA tournament. If you lose, there is no other game. I don't know if that scares you or excites you. Either way, it's reality."

Like the springtime, our team is beginning anew. This is the time of the year when we not only must be playing our best basketball, but when we should be our most enthusiastic about playing. So I'll talk to the team about having just run a long race, about having to renew ourselves for the big push of the postseason.

"It's been a long season, guys, and we need to get refreshed. And I tell you what we're going to do. We're going to clear our heads, rest and recharge our batteries, and then we're going to get after it."

As the leader of our team, I'm now looking very carefully at the demeanor of my team. Are we healthy, are we injured? Are we excited, are we down? Are we energized, are we tired?

Some leaders stay up in the ivory tower and dictate what the team needs to do next without knowing specifically how the team is feeling or what they want. Well, I not only like to be around our team as much as possible so that I can observe them, I also like to pull one of the captains aside to ask his opinion.

"Wojo, what do you think?"

"I think we're pretty tired, Coach."

"Are *you* tired?"

"Yeah, Coach, I'm tired."

Well, if Wojciechowski ever told me he was tired, I knew the entire team was really tired. Because Wojo had more energy than anyone else. That's one reason he was selected captain.

So, after conferring with our assistant coaches, we may decide to give the players a day off. Or we might bring them in, show them five minutes of tape, have some pizza and ice cream, and then tell them to "get outta here and have some fun." Now a kid might want to stay and shoot some baskets on

139

his own, and that's okay. But we're not going to coach them today. We'll coach them tomorrow.

The general idea during this renewal phase is to determine what the team needs right now and then provide it for them. We also have to start preparing for each phase of the tournament. All teams will play on a Thursday-Saturday or Friday-Sunday schedule. We have to determine which schedule we're on and then we have to take into consideration travel time. Are we traveling out west or do we stay east? And then when do we hold practices? Shall we practice hard on Monday and Tuesday or should we wait until Wednesday or Thursday? We don't want to start a mile run with a 100 yard dash. Nor do we wait too long to begin our final kick. However we handle it, it will depend mostly on the team itself.

But I'll give them a lot of help. I'll remind them that throughout the regular season, we believed we could win. And that our formula consisted of preparation, communication, hard work, practice, and focus—which will continue to be our guide.

We will also try to get them to remember how well they played during the regular season. Our staff might put together a short highlight tape of good things that happened during some of our better winning streaks. Big plays, great offensive and defensive efforts, diving for loose balls, taking the key charge, things like that. The idea is to put the players in a confident and positive frame of mind so that they will be prepared for the first round of the tournament.

Our Duke teams generally earn a fairly high seed in our region—number three, number two, sometimes even number one. As a result, our first-round opponent is a low seed, which means we're heavily favored to win the game. But how we win, how we set the stage for the rest of the tournament, is key in the first round.

In preparation for that first game, then, we will not concentrate so much on Xs and Os as much as we will focus on personnel and qualities that forge winners—things like effort, determination, and dominance.

"If we play poorly in the first game and win it," I'll ask the players, "is that okay?"

"Uh, no."

"No, it's not okay. Because we might play at ten on Thursday night and then have a Saturday game at noon. So if we play poorly on Thursday, we have only thirty-six hours to get ready for our next opponent. Well, that next opponent will be better and more capable of beating us. So we do not—I repeat, we *do not* want to let that first game put us in a bad situation performance-wise. We want to be on a high level going into that second game."

At this point, I will remind the players how, during the regular season, we intentionally scheduled a few tough games at times that would be similar to the NCAA tournament.

"Remember that game we scheduled at Madison Square Garden on a Sunday against St. John's? And then how we had to turn right around and play North Carolina? Well, what did we ask you to do after the St. John's game? Get a good night's sleep, remember? And then we practiced, prepared, and focused. We put that St. John's game behind us very quickly. We won both of those games then—and we can do it again now."

Essentially, I remind our team that we've already done this stuff before. It's nothing new. The regular season was kind of like a rehearsal for the postseason.

And just like we set mini-goals for ourselves over short periods of time, we'll have additional "energy bursts" for the

NCAA tournament. We'll focus on the small four-team brackets, rather than the huge bracket that centers on the Final Four. In our region, wherever our site is, we have to win the first game, play the second game, then win the second game. If we do that, then we will define our next goal.

In essence, then, we look at the entire tournament as a series of four-team tournaments—each one lasting one week in duration. So wherever we are geographically, we'll give the players a copy of only the four-team bracket for that week. And I'll tell them:

"Focus on nothing else. Don't worry about the Sweet Sixteen, the Elite Eight, or the Final Four. Be careful to focus on one game at a time. We don't want to look ahead and worry about which team we might play in the second game and how we might defend against them. One team at a time. One game at a time. Then next game—fast. If we do that well, we'll go a long way."

Media and Public Relations

In preparation for the tournament, we also talk to the players about the media. We remind them of our policies during the regular season, which, for the most part, will also apply now. Treat members of the media with respect. Be honest and open with them, but don't tell them every detail of our existence. There will be an open locker room after every game. Each player is on his own to answer questions to anybody who asks.

This is exactly how we handle things during the regular season. It prepares the players not only for March Madness, but for life after Duke—whether it's in the NBA or in business.

Jay Bilas, for instance, once remarked that, in being coached to tell the press the truth, he learned a valuable lesson that he applies in his professional career as both a trial lawyer and a sports broadcaster.

"There are times in business," he said, "when you'll make a mistake. When that happens, you have to deal with it straightforwardly. You have to be accountable and step up and say, 'Yes, this is what happened.' Essentially, I tell the truth. If you're operating on the truth, you'll do well. If you're operating on anything less, you're dead. I learned that from Coach K at Duke."

In any given year, we play around forty games, including exhibitions and scrimmages. So forty times in the locker room after games, our players have anywhere from five to twenty microphones and cameras in their faces—for four years. I don't believe there's another place in America where young people can get that kind of on-the-job training with the media.

My philosophy is that we should not cut players off from interviews. It is a tremendous experience for them to be able to learn how to deal with the media. As a matter of fact, I think some consideration should be given to providing the students with course credits for their efforts. If they make some mistakes, that's okay. They have to stumble a few times to grow up. I don't believe in sheltering them. That's not the real world.

But we don't necessarily throw them to the wolves and let them be eaten alive, either. Over the course of the regular season, we'll work with them. We'll critique their interviews together and discuss what went well and what they could do better next time. And we'll direct them to answer questions regarding the game they just played rather than getting into some other areas that might lead to disharmony on the team.

For example, we might advise them to not discuss relationships with their teammates or the details of what happens in our practices. Essentially, our team is a work in progress. In building relationships, a player might not be as tight with a teammate as he would be a month down the road. That's natural. Everybody doesn't just come together right away, meet on a mountaintop, and embrace. That's not the way it happens. The players on our team are succeeding together and they're failing together. Relationships can change rapidly. But the media doesn't understand that. I'm not sure the players completely understand it. At any rate, it can't be explained in any one interview.

During the NCAA tournament, everything with the media is magnified, due in large part to a billion-dollar contract with CBS that provides over 80 percent of the NCAA's total revenue. As a result, a lot of coaches are always being asked if they can put a microphone on us. "Can we put a mike in your huddle? Can we interview you at halftime? Can we come into your locker room?"

My answer is always, "No. No way."

At halftime, going into the locker room, or coming back out to start the second half, I don't want to give a TV interview because the game is still going on. Just because there's a break in the action doesn't mean I'm not completely and totally focused on the task at hand. That's just my personal preference. I'm still concentrating on the game because of my commitment to our team.

In addition, there are certain things the media has no business being involved in. Our locker room during those moments is a very special place. It is meant for our group alone, no one else. I'm not going to let television cameras come in during a Christmas dinner or a family discussion. You don't allow somebody to sit in on a private candlelight dinner with your wife, do you? Well, I don't want anybody to ruin that time we have together. That's *our* private time. We need it. And we're going to have it.

Besides, I'm not sure we would all be honest with each other if we were hooked up to a microphone during a game. If we're having a tough go of it, for instance, would there be full disclosure, would there be total and absolute honesty and instant truth? Probably not. And that alone would hurt the performance and unity of the team.

And I'm also concerned about disturbing the purity of the game. I think it goes back to my days on the playground with the Columbos. We didn't play for acclaim or adulation or money. We played for the pure enjoyment of it. And we played because we were friends, because we were with each other, and because it's a great game.

I'm strong about that and I want my players to see that I'm strong about it. I think, then, that we'll have a greater chance of playing for innocence.

Believe but Don't Assume

Going into the NCAA tournament, I will ask our group how many teams feel that they can win it all.

Some will respond, "All the teams."

Others will say, "Well, half the teams."

"No, guys," I'll reply, "how many teams *really, truly* believe they can win this tournament?"

And the answers will be varied: "Eight, five, three, two?"

"Fellas, there are probably less than a handful of teams who believe they can win it all. Most don't believe they can

145

win. Some are just happy to have been selected. And they should be. A 17-13 team should be thrilled to have made it to the Big Dance. And they'll have a lot of fun just being there, just competing. There'll be other teams who have the goal of making it to the Sweet Sixteen or to the Elite Eight. Others will hope and dream that they can make it to the Final Four. But *most* of the teams will not believe they can win it all."

Then I will pause in my remarks to the team so that I make certain every one of the players is looking me straight in the eye.

"Gentlemen, we have to be one of the teams who believes we can win it all," I'll tell them. "It's true we belong in the tournament. We've earned the right to be a high seed because of the way we played during the regular season. All our hard work has paid off. But more important than simply believing we belong is believing we can win."

Then I will caution the team about taking winning for granted. They will be under a lot of pressure, as all their friends and families may be already saying that Duke is going to the Final Four. Because we've had success in the past, there's a tendency simply to assume that we'll have success again.

"Guys, one of *the* worst things anybody can do is assume," I'll say to the team. "I think fools assume. If people have *really* got it together, they never assume anything. They believe, they work hard, and they prepare—but they don't assume.

"All year long, I've talked to you about respecting your opponent—all year long, whether we're playing South Carolina State or Maryland, St. John's or Army. That's why I've asked you to dive for loose balls whether we're down by 20, up by 20, or tied. It didn't matter who we were playing. We wanted to play at a high level of excellence.

"The tournament is the reason why. Now that we're here, we're not going to overlook our first-round or second-round opponents. We're going to respect them. If we were to disrespect our competition, we would be disrespecting ourselves."

So I tell our team that we belong in the tournament. The whole year has been preparation for the month of March. We must go in with confidence, courage, and pride. And I tell them to believe they *can* win, but don't assume they *will* win.

We must have respect for each opponent we play—from the first round to the national championship game. One at a time, we prepare and we play our best basketball. Then it's on to the next team.

And after each and every game, we're 0-0 again.

It's the only way.

Coach K's Tips

- Take time to get refreshed. Clear your head, rest and recharge your batteries, and then get after it.

- Look very carefully at the demeanor of your team. Are they healthy, injured, excited, down, energized, or tired?

- Ask your team leaders their opinions.

- Let your formula of preparation, communication, hard work, practice, and focus continue to be your guide.

- Set mini-goals. Plan for "energy bursts."

- In the first round, how you win, how you set the stage, is key.

- Treat members of the media with respect. Be honest and open with them, but don't tell them every detail of your existence.

- Be one of the teams who believes you can win it all. But don't assume that you *will* win it all.

- Always respect your competition. To disrespect your competition is to disrespect yourself.

10

HANDLING A CRISIS

"I believe God gave us crises for some reason—and it certainly wasn't for us to say that everything about them is bad. A crisis can be a momentous time for a team to grow—if a leader handles it properly."

—Coach K

"When we won that last-second game over Kentucky, many people said we were lucky. But I think luck favors teams who trust one another."

—Coach K

"A leader has to show the face his team needs to see."

—Coach K

*I*t's Kentucky 103, Duke 102.

With 2.1 seconds left in overtime.

Grant Hill takes the ball out of bounds under the Kentucky basket.

He throws the ball the length of the court.

Christian Laettner's coming across. He catches it at the top of the key.

He dribbles. He turns. He jumps. He shoots.

Time runs out while the ball's in the air.

It's . . . gooooooood!!!!!

Duke wins! Duke wins!

Kids on playgrounds across America still reenact the end of our big win against Kentucky in the East Regional championship game of March 1992. That game meant everything to us because the winner would go on to the Final Four. So when we found ourselves down by one point with 2.1 seconds left in overtime, it was a major crisis. And we were fortunate to pull out a victory in what many people have called the greatest single game in the history of college basketball.

I believe a crisis occurs when it means the most. In business, if you encounter a last-second problem in a $100 deal, it's not really a crisis. But if a hitch occurs at the end of a billion-dollar deal, it's a *huge* crisis.

And the worse the crisis is, the more people tend to act as individuals rather than as members of a team. They just naturally think, "I'm dead," not necessarily, "We're dead." And rather than looking for opportunities, the tendency is to deflate and say, "It's over. I'm going to have to find another job because the company won't be here in a couple of months. Time to look out for old number one."

I believe God gave us crises for some reason—and it certainly isn't for us to say that everything about them is bad. A crisis can be a momentous time for a team to grow—if a leader handles it properly. Think of all the towns around the country that have experienced a flood, a fire, a hurricane, a tornado. Effective leadership can help a community become closer, tighter. When the river's going to overflow, you can see people who normally never even speak to one another filling sandbags together, passing them to one another in long lines, and then stacking them up high to protect their homes. In a crisis, a leader demonstrates that people need one another. And, all of a sudden, the town they live in can rise to a whole different level of friendship and spirituality.

In basketball, my line of work, we frequently have moments of crisis. How we handle each situation, what we do in such moments, has a lot to do with our success or failure as a team.

What is it that leaders do in a crisis situation? They stay

calm, stay focused, stay positive, stay confident, and utilize their best people.

We've all heard this kind of advice before. It's pretty standard in a business situation. And, of course, staying calm, focused, and confident is extremely important—as is utilizing the talents of your best personnel. And so is looking at the positive side of things—to make something great out of something potentially disastrous. But success in handling a crisis situation depends to a very large extent on what has developed (or not developed) prior to the crisis ever taking place.

Truth and Trusting Relationships

When we won that last-second game over Kentucky, many people said we were lucky. But I think luck favors teams who trust one another.

One of the things that helped us was the fact that we were already a close, tight-knit group of people. And, in that very tough situation, we were able to take advantage of the close relationships we had built. Long before we stepped on the court with Kentucky, the trust was already there. When I told the guys what I felt they needed to hear, they knew it was the truth. I had successfully established that all-important principle that every coach strives for—"instant belief."

Over time, I was able to build up to it, in part, by admitting that I was wrong when I screwed up. A leader has to show that he's real, that he can make a mistake. Because if the members of the team are supposed to see themselves through the leader's eyes, so does the leader have to see himself as others see him.

When a leader makes a mistake and doesn't admit it, he is

seen as arrogant or untrustworthy. And "untrustworthy" is the last thing a leader wants to be. Accordingly, I will apologize to a member of the team if I make a mistake.

I remember one time I chewed out a player in practice, but after I reviewed the videotape, I found that the kid was playing his position in the correct manner. So at the next practice, I went up to him.

"Billy, that was stupid of me. I shouldn't have said that."

"Oh, Coach, it's cool. It's okay."

"Nope. That wasn't right. I'm sorry."

Another time, I asked a player to play a certain way in a game. Well, when he did exactly what I asked him to do, it didn't work. In fact, it made both him and the team look awful. So, at halftime, I apologized to the kid in front of the entire team.

"You know, when I came in here before the ball game, I was an idiot," I said. "We're getting beat because I ordered you to do the wrong thing. Well, I want all of you to look at me. I am not an idiot anymore. You're not being led by an idiot. So let's get our heads out of our rear ends because I put them there for you. Let's start playing the way we all know we can play."

I've gotten better at admitting my mistakes over the years. And I believe some of it comes from being with Mickie and our daughters. From them, I've learned that to admit a mistake is not a weakness, it's a strength. As a matter of fact, it shows confidence in the relationship. "I messed up. I'm sorry. I won't do that again. Let's go on from here."

People are not going to follow you as a leader unless you show them that you're real. They are not going to believe you unless they trust you. And they are not going to trust you unless you always tell them the truth and admit when you were wrong.

If you get into a crisis and you have no trust among the members of your team, then you might be in a hopeless situation. Successful crisis management is best achieved when people are truthful with one another—immediately.

Have Fun

There are many end-of-regular-season tournaments. But the Atlantic Coast Conference tournament is the granddaddy of them all. In fact, it started a tradition that has since been copied by other basketball conferences across the country.

The tournament is a four-day happening to celebrate ACC basketball. There are no public sales of tickets. As a matter of fact, people put the tickets in their wills and pass them on to future generations.

The winner of the tournament is the official champion of the Atlantic Coast Conference. As a result, there is a lot of pressure on all the participants. And that pressure only intensifies for any team that is fortunate to advance.

Whether you win or lose, it is a taxing period of time. There's neighborhood pressure for bragging rights. But there's also national pressure for positioning in the NCAA tournament. An early loss could drop a team in the seedings.

When the tournament first started, only the winner went to the NCAA tournament—and no one else could go. But when those rules were changed to allow other teams to be picked for the NCAA tournament, the intensity and pressure of the ACC tournament did not wane.

In 1988, we were playing our archrival, North Carolina, in

the championship game. We had beaten them twice that year—and they were out for revenge. It was a particularly tough game, close all the way. In the second half, UNC took a 55–50 lead, but our defense picked up its intensity to force the Tar Heels to come up empty on 16 of the final 19 trips down the court.

With four seconds left to play and Duke clinging to a 63–61 lead, Quin Snyder was fouled going for a loose ball. A timeout was called and when our players came to the bench and sat down, I could see in their faces that they were tense and worried.

"C'mon, guys," I said. "Here's what I want you to do. Just sit here. Just feel the moment. Listen to the crowd. Feel the enthusiasm.

"Isn't this great?" I said. "Why are you putting pressure on yourselves? Isn't this fun? Isn't it wonderful? I want you to enjoy it. I want you to *remember* it."

We didn't talk about any strategy in that huddle. All I said was, "Quin, just relax. You've got 'em. Okay?"

And Quin went back out there, shot his two free throws, hit them both, and we won the ACC championship to complete a rare three-game season sweep of the Tar Heels.

That was another crisis situation. It was a championship game and we had to have those two free throws. But there was so much tension among the team that I felt they needed to purge it from themselves so they wouldn't expend all their energy worrying—especially Quin Snyder. I really wanted them to enjoy themselves because having fun helps reduce pressure. And there is always pressure in an emergency situation.

There also tends to be some pressure when preparing for the Big Dance—the NCAA tournament. When you get to a certain point in the season, you've got to have some other reasons for playing the game. So why not approach it where you have some fun? That's why in practices, I'll often goof with the players. I'll make jokes. I'll have a little fun with the guys. After all, I don't want them to see me with furrows in my forehead all the time.

I recall one time during the 1992 season when I was trying to build up Grant Hill's confidence. I wanted Grant to be more instinctive. He was thinking too much and I wanted him to go with his natural talents, to play more by feel. So in a team meeting, I started talking about how effective Grant was because of his mental approach to the game. Then I started goofing around with Bobby Hurley.

"Bobby, will you tell him you don't think about anything?"

As the team began laughing, Hurley got this sheepish, little-boy grin on his face and finally began to laugh himself. And after they all calmed down, I made a certain point so that Grant would stay pumped up and Bobby wouldn't have his feelings hurt.

"Bobby doesn't get tired because he's not analyzing," I told the guys. "He's like a great chef who doesn't use a recipe, he just cooks by feel. But we'll take you the way you are, Bobby, because the best thing you do is win—just like Grant."

Another time, when the team was struggling and had lost a few games in a row near the end of the regular season, the team was gathered in the locker room for my standard pregame talk.

Well, I turned out the lights and walked in with a lighted candle in my hand.

"I'm just an old Polish coach looking for a few players with heart," I said.

That was my entire pregame oration. And all of the players who were in the locker room that day still talk about it.

I don't plan things like that. I kind of do them by feel—
when the moment seems right. I think the guys who've played
for me over the years would tell you that I have a good sense
of humor. I've always tried to show it because I want all the
players to have fun during their time at Duke. It's part of being
on the journey. We need to enjoy it.

Show the Face Your Team Needs to See

A leader also has to show the face his team needs to see.
Because, before he ever utters a word, they see his face. They
also see his eyes, even his walk.

I'm always aware of how I enter a room. Before a game, I
might walk into the locker room quickly, with a spring in my
step and a smile on my face. And as I come in, I might say
something like: "Hey, we're going to be really good tonight. In
fact, we might be *great* tonight."

Whatever I say after that will not be as important as how I
look to them.

"Did he really mean it?"

"Yeah, look at his face. He really meant it. We might be
great tonight."

A good leader presents an image that gives confidence to
his team. And I make it a point to transform that image to the
players by encouraging them to walk right, to stand right, to
look good.

"If you want to be a really good player," I tell them, "you
have to walk like a good player."

This is a principle I learned at West Point, a school where
each cadet majors in leadership. Show your team that you're
worthy to lead them. Stand tall. Stay stoic or smile as the situ-

157

ation warrants. Keep your face clean. Keep your uniform clean. Don't show any mud on your shoes. Portray an image that can give your team whatever they may need at that moment: a smile, a frown, emotion, anger, a joke.

Some of the things a leader has to conquer are human emotions like fear. And you do not necessarily beat fear with a hug. Sometimes you just have to attack the hell out of it. Human things have to be approached in different ways. It's not always wise to storm up the hill and attack the machine gun.

Confidence, of course, can be an extremely effective weapon against fear. When I'm in competition, I don't want to ever let my opponents see us get hurt, see us down, or see us worried. If we show our emotions, where they see they're getting to us, it'll give *them* more confidence. By showing confidence in ourselves, even in moments of crisis, we become stronger. So I always advise the players on our team to: "Show confidence, hide weakness."

And for aspiring leaders, I advise: "Whether you completely believe it or not, you must have the expression on your face and the words in your mouth that the team *is going to win.*"

Trying to Get to Heaven

The big pearl in the NCAA tournament is the regional championship game. It's like the NFC or the AFC championship games in pro football. If you win, you're going to the Super Bowl. Well, if you win the regional championship at the Big Dance, you go to the Super Bowl of college basketball—the Final Four.

Every coach and every player dreams about going there. It's Mecca. It's Utopia. A career is defined by being able to say that you made it to one, two, or several Final Fours. Of course, everyone wants to win the national championship. That's the best. But not everybody can identify with the national championship. Everybody, however, can identify with going to the Final Four. It's at the center of all the brackets that people have been studying and following and filling out. It's almost like the tournament is played to get to the Final Four.

So if we're fortunate to make it to that regional championship game, we know that anything can happen—anything. I believe it's the biggest game of the year—filled to the brim with pressure, tension, and spectacle. When you go into that game, you wonder, Who is going to make it to Mecca? Who is going to heaven? And you hope you're the one.

The biggest and most memorable of all the regional finals I've been a part of was the Duke-Kentucky contest in March of 1992 before a sellout crowd at the Spectrum in Philadelphia.

Kentucky had played a terrific game to beat UMass in the semifinals. They had a great coach in Rick Pitino, a talented sophomore in Jamal Mashburn, and four tough, seasoned seniors. After Duke outlasted Seton Hall in our semifinal game, we knew it was not going to be any picnic to have to turn right around and go up against Kentucky only two days later. And, man, what a contest it was.

Early in the game, the teams played fairly evenly. But after we had deadlocked at 20–20, Duke began to move ahead. We took a lead into the locker room at halftime and led by as much as 12 points midway through the second half. But Kentucky stormed back with the help of a 9–0 run behind the inspired play of Mashburn. And at the end of regulation, the score was knotted at 93.

159

In the overtime period, Kentucky jumped out to a small lead, but we fought back to tie it. Then we started matching basket for basket, foul shot for foul shot. And it looked like the last team with the ball was going to the Final Four.

With 7.8 seconds left on the clock, and Duke leading by one point, 102–101, Rick Pitino called a timeout to set up a play. Senior Richie Farmer inbounded the ball to his classmate Sean Woods, who drove the ball to the right of the foul line.

Bobby Hurley fell to the floor after being taken out by a solid screen. But Laettner came over to cover and Woods tossed up a "Hail Mary" over Christian's extended arms.

By all rights, that shot should not have gone in the basket because of Laettner's great defensive effort. But, somehow, the ball bounced off the backboard and went through the hoop, giving Kentucky a 103–102 lead.

It was an unbelievable shot—unconventional and terrific. But it made me angry. I didn't want to lose this big game, after we had played so well, so courageously, on a shot like that! There was no way Woods had intended to bank that ball head-on into the basket. And now, I was afraid that our guys would think that this just wasn't their day—it just wasn't meant to be.

I was so mad I threw a towel on the ground and signaled for a timeout with 2.1 seconds left. Anger is okay if it motivates you to do something good. Sometimes anger destroys fear. And I wanted our players to be angry, too.

But they weren't. They were shell-shocked—knocked back like a hard punch to the face would do.

As they walked back from the other side of the court, I saw their dazed looks and I noticed that they were physically apart. It was clear to me that they were thinking individually—as people tend to do in a crisis.

Hurley could have been thinking that if Laettner would

have blocked that shot, we wouldn't be in this situation. Laettner might have been thinking if Hurley had done a better job guarding that guy, he wouldn't have made the basket. Grant Hill, I found out later, was wondering what beach he was going to be on next week because he sure wasn't going to be playing in the Final Four.

In a crisis situation like this, I instinctively realized that I had to get them to snap out of the daze they were in and I had to make them believe, positively, that they could win this game. Then I had to get them all singing out of the same hymnal. And it all had to be done in less than two minutes.

So when we got the timeout, I didn't wait for them to come to the bench. I walked out on the court to meet them. They saw my confident walk before they heard me speak. They saw my face before they ever heard my words.

When they got close to me, their eyes told me that they could not win.

"We're going to win!" I said immediately. "We're going to win!"

Then I motioned them over to take their seats on the bench and I knelt down in front of them at eye level. And I said it again, as they all looked squarely at me.

"We are going to win! Do you understand? We are going to win!"

It was like being in the emergency room with a heart attack patient and putting the electric pads on his chest.

"We are going to win! Poomf! We are going to win! Poomf! Wake up! Poomf! Come back to life! Poomf!"

Finally, they came back to life. They heard me. Finally I could see in their eyes that they were over the shock.

In a crisis, it appears to most people that there are no opportunities. But a leader's job is to create opportunities. A

161

leader has to find a way to win—and *believe* he can win. And, that day, I really did believe we were going to win. I believed this group of young men could do anything. I was that confident in them.

So I instantly thought up a play.

Now they had to believe me. They had to believe that the play would work, that there was, in fact, still time to win this game.

So I involved them in the conversation and got them talking to me.

"Grant, we need a three-quarter-court pass. Grant, can you make the pass?"

"Yeah, Coach. I can do it."

"Christian, you're going to flash from the left corner to the top of the key. Christian, can you catch it?"

Laettner nodded that he could.

Then, as I diagrammed the play, I positioned Thomas Hill at half-court on the opposite sideline—and Tony Lang under the basket. If Christian couldn't catch the pass, he would try to tip it to Thomas. If he got the shot off and missed, Tony could tip it in. I also positioned Hurley at midcourt in case Grant couldn't hit Christian with a pass. Then he could throw it to Bobby, who would have to improvise from there.

"Christian," I asked once again, "can you do it?"

"If Grant can throw it, I can catch it and hit the shot."

"Good! Now remember, guys, the clock doesn't start until Christian has touched the ball. We still have 2.1 seconds left."

Finally, just before our players went out onto the court, we joined hands together and again reaffirmed to one another: "We're going to win!"

And when they left the huddle, their eyes now told me that we had a chance. They were confident, they were positive, they were together, and they were armed with a good plan.

Grant Hill positioned himself under the basket for the throw in. Then the whistle blew and he threw the ball 75 feet to the top of the key at the other end of the court.

Christian Laettner came across from the left side.

It was like a beautiful pass in football with the receiver in motion and the quarterback putting it right on the money, right where he knew his teammate would be.

Laettner caught the ball at the top of the key. He knew he had 2.1 seconds.

He dribbled the ball twice to set up his move.

He turned. He jumped. He took his shot.

Time ran out on the clock as the ball was in the air.

It swished through the net in slow motion.

Pandemonium. Joy. Despair. Disbelief.

Thomas Hill held his head and said: "Oh, my God!"

The final score was: Duke 104, Kentucky 103.

We had won and we were headed to heaven—but I just sat there. I did not jump up and down for joy. As a matter of fact, I never even saw the ball go into the basket.

Rather, I was looking at the faces of the players. First Christian's face—and I just knew the shot would be good. Then my line of sight shifted to Richie Farmer, a senior for Kentucky who I knew had just finished his last game. I saw his face—the hurt, the shock, the utter despair. So I went to him, put my arm around him, tried to console him.

My job isn't just to win basketball games, it is to lead my team, to take care of my men. And that kind of leadership is ongoing. So my responsibility was not going to end on that last shot—especially if the ball had not gone in the basket. If we had lost, my heart was going to have to go out to my team to console the players. But as it happened, they did not need me. So I instinctively tried to help the first person I saw who needed help—Richie Farmer.

And then, after shaking hands with Rick Pitino, Kentucky's great head coach, I walked over to the Kentucky press table and spoke on the air with Cawood Ledford, the legendary radio play-by-play announcer for the Wildcats.

"Please," I said to all the Kentucky fans who were listening in, "be proud of your team. Give them the welcome home they deserve. They've represented you in the best possible way."

Coach K's Tips

- The worse the crisis, the more people will tend to think as individuals rather than as members of a team.

- Luck favors teams who trust one another.

- When you screw up, admit you are wrong. Apologize in front of the whole team. To admit a mistake is not a weakness, it's a strength.

- Successful crisis management is best achieved when people are truthful with one another—immediately.

- Having fun helps reduce pressure.

- Maintain a good sense of humor. You don't always want your team to see you with furrows in your forehead.

- Before you ever utter a word, the team sees your face, the look in your eyes, even your walk. Show the face your team needs to see.

- You do not necessarily beat fear with a hug. Sometimes you have to attack the hell out of it.

- Confidence can be an extremely effective weapon against fear. Show strength, hide weakness.

- Anger is okay if it motivates you to do something good.

- A leader's job is to create opportunities. A leader has to find a way to win.

11

FOCUS ON THE TASK AT HAND

"I don't think I have to apologize for us getting to the Final Four three or four times and not winning. I'd rather play and be beaten than not be there at all."

—Coach K

"A leader's responsibility to his team is paramount. It overshadows even his own personal feelings at any given time."

—Coach K

"I believe a big part of leadership is about winning the moment."

—Coach K

*I*n 1990, our season ended with a loss in Denver, Colorado.

Actually, it was more than a loss. We were blown out in the national championship game by the University of Nevada at Las Vegas by a score of 103–73—the highest scoring margin in the history of NCAA tournament championship games.

When the media asked me after the game what I would have done differently, I replied: "Well, I could have showed up with a different team, or they could have had a different coach, or UNLV could have gotten sick." Essentially, I offered no excuses.

Back at the hotel that evening, Mickie and I were sitting around with members of our coaching staff when my mother walked in with my brother and sister-in-law.

"*Mike!*" my mom shouted out. "Don't *worry!* You'll do better next year!"

So I sat there for a moment trying to rationalize. Let's see. We had a great year. We made it to the Final Four, played in the national championship game. Hmmm. There's only one way I can do better next year and that's to win it all.

"Mom," I said. "I know you're just trying to make me feel better. But you can't do a whole lot better than this. C'mon."

"You'll do *better*," she said again.

The Final Four

When you make it to the Final Four, everybody around you is happy. Players and coaches are happy. Parents are happy. Fans are happy. Everybody's happy. Maybe that's why they call it the Big Dance.

There is also incredible excitement and activity. As a matter of fact, just being at the Final Four sometimes overshadows the national championship.

The media ratchets up all their attention a notch. Camera crews follow the teams around and there always seems to be a microphone stuck in your face. Now they're not just looking for stories, they're looking for angles. What about those two walk-ons for Duke who were former managers? What about that UCLA guy who works with poor kids in Nicaragua? Isn't there a player with UConn who had some sort of family crisis?

The distractions are unbelievable at the Final Four. Part of the reason is that CBS and the NCAA have that billion-dollar TV contract that, in part, stipulates specific requirements that teams must participate in. On the first night, for example, there is a salute presentation for the local organizing committee. The four head coaches have to be present and speak. As the week progresses, an inordinate amount of interviews are

169

required. There's a press conference on this day. The starting team has to be there. At the beginning of your practice sessions, the players have to spend forty-five minutes with the press. The locker room has to be open for thirty minutes. The head coach has to do a thirty-minute interview with CBS Radio, for CBS TV, and then another thirty minutes with the print media. In all, we end up being in the gym three hours for a fifty-minute practice session.

It's like going to the Super Bowl with all the pregame hype—except that we don't have professional athletes. We have college kids dealing with it all. So there's a tendency for our team to be pulled apart a little bit—whether it's me not being with the team or a few of the players being highlighted individually.

Normally, I'm not separated from our team much when we're on the road. Even the majority of postseason tournament play is not all that different. But during the Final Four, all of a sudden, I'm pulled away from my team. I can't be with them for all the team meals. We lose our private moments before practice. There's not as much time for one-on-one conversations.

The magnitude of the event separates us from one another and we can start to feel distance between us. Things can get messed up a little bit. We begin thinking about things other than our upcoming game. We can lose our edge. I think the more tight-knit a team is, the more impact the hoopla of the Final Four can have. It's just tougher to keep the group close.

For this last week of the postseason, the train is really full. A lot of people have jumped on board. And the distractions are multiplied and magnified.

So, how do we handle it all?

Well, first of all, I delegate as much as possible. I turn over all the details of the Final Four media to Mike Cragg, our sports information director. He has to get his armored suit out to handle all the bullets coming Duke's way. He has to keep us all informed, reminded, and organized about all the media requirements and commitments. There's no way I could do all that myself. Nor would I want to. Every free moment has to be dedicated to preparing our team for the game.

Another person I depend on greatly is my executive assistant, Gerry Brown, who also has to have a suit of armor. That's because she handles the most coveted of all items—tickets to the Final Four.

Everybody wants to go. And now they know somebody who's going—a player, a coach, a manager, a member of the staff. "Hey, I went to high school with that guy. I wonder if he remembers me? He's got to remember me. Of course, I'll get a ticket." Everybody on the team gets hit up by classmates they don't remember and cousins they didn't know they had.

And of course, we never have enough tickets. So Gerry handles it all. Members of the team get their requests to her and she says yes or no for everybody. Now, that might not seem like such a big deal. But when you're trying to keep a team together and on track for their next game, all these requests for tickets can present a huge obstacle. And it's my job as the team's leader to remove any obstacle that can impact our team's performance. So I delegate the ticket and media tasks to people I trust completely.

I also depend a great deal on our assistant coaches to pick up some of the slack while I'm diverted to other commitments. They will all spend extra time with the players and keep an eye on them for me. They'll be ready to advise me when I ask questions. "How were the kids with the press?

What were they doing in the locker room? Have I missed some of the telltale signs that will give me a hint of where their heads are? Are they ready, not ready, scared, excited? Where are they, Johnny? I haven't been able to look in their eyes!"

And the players themselves have to pick up some of the slack and take responsibility for their performance. Their focus and concentration have to be supreme. We've been working on our focus all year long, so it should be pretty sharp by now.

The kids have been in front of the media for more than thirty games. They should be prepared.

We've played big games in front of thousands of screaming people at Madison Square Garden, the Meadowlands, at North Carolina. They should be prepared.

We've been preparing all year for this moment. We all should be prepared.

Winning the Moment

A leader's responsibility to his team is paramount. It overshadows even his own personal feelings at any given time.

At the Final Four, I may be worried or upset or concerned that all of the media hype is destroying our team unity. But I will not allow myself to show those feelings to the group. I have to be strong enough to say to myself, "That's not allowed. That would be violating my commitment to them. I'm not allowed to feel sorry for myself right now. I'm not allowed to be down. I'm not allowed to be angry. I'm not allowed to be weak right now."

Because I know that these people are dependent on me, I beat back the emotion that I feel. This particular personal determination I have reminds me of my mom—who would never allow my brother and me to know that we were poor when we were growing up. She just wasn't going to let us worry about it. I never knew we were poor. I never even *thought* about us being poor. We didn't have a car. We didn't have a house. We didn't have money. And if it ever bothered her, it never showed to her kids. And I can't let my players know if I'm troubled about something personally.

A leader should strive to do his best 100 percent of the time. That's why I try to eliminate all obstacles, both personal and mental, that might prevent our team from doing its best. As a result, I'm always asking myself the important question: "Okay, what does this group need right now?"

Leadership, like basketball, is a game of adjustments. If a leader is too structured, he'll be unable to adjust quickly—unable to seize the moment with decisiveness and creativity. And, basically, I believe a big part of leadership is about winning the moment.

There was no more important a "moment" than the one we experienced at the 1991 Final Four at the Hoosier Dome in Indianapolis. In my entire coaching career, that was the forty-eight hours I'm most proud of. We had been to the three previous Final Fours and had not "won it all," as some people liked to remind me.

But I was determined not to let thinking like that affect my performance or attitude. I don't think I have to apologize for us getting to the Final Four three or four times and not winning. I'd rather play and be beaten than not be there at all.

But in 1991, we had a particularly tough road ahead of us—especially in the first game. We were up against the undefeated and top-ranked team in the nation, the University of Nevada at Las Vegas. They had not lost a game since well before they pummeled us by 30 points in the championship game the year before. They had not trailed in a game all year. Their average margin of victory was 25 points. Not only had they won 45 games in a row, they were picked by everybody to absolutely destroy us again. According to all the experts, we didn't have a chance. All Duke could hope for was a respectable showing.

Well, I knew the UNLV Runnin' Rebels were a really good basketball team. In fact, I knew they were better than the 1990 team that beat us—but they weren't all that much better. And even though we were a relatively young team, I was certain that we were a heck of a lot better than we were when we lost to them by 30 points.

So I knew we had more than a chance to win. As a matter of fact, I was certain we could win the game if we could stay close in the early going. And I told the team as much. But I also told them not to listen to the media or what was printed in the papers. "Don't even listen to what I say publicly," I also said. "Just listen to what I tell you face-to-face." Then I went out and portrayed us in the media as the poor underdogs.

In order for us to win, however, I knew it would take more than blowing a little smoke the media's way. It would also take unbelievable focus and concentration. And it would take tremendous discipline for us to overcome all the inherent distractions of the Final Four. The 1991 UNLV game would have to be a defining moment for us, I believed. It would have to be a line-in-the-sand game.

My theme for that entire week was not only that we could win, but that we were destined to win. "This is *our* time," I kept telling the players—both individually and as a group. I was trying to get over any possibilities where anyone might rationalize that it was okay to lose if we played hard and came close.

I did not tell the team that the mere fact we were in the Final Four was a victory. No. I told them that this was our time to win the national championship. This time. Not next time. Not next year. This year. Now.

I also carefully studied the 1990 loss to UNLV on videotape. I noticed that whenever UNLV challenged us, we backed down. I observed a sick Bobby Hurley, a tired team overall. Even I looked hollow. I saw no fire in Duke's head coach on the sidelines. And I vowed that it would be different this time.

I had short individual videotapes made from the past season's games (and the UNLV loss) of our players that highlighted positive things about them—good passes, great shots, super defense. And then I showed them to each player individually so that they would feel good about themselves. Each kid saw his video twice—once before we left for Indianapolis and once just before the game. So in the locker room waiting to play UNLV, all the players and coaches were watching the first game of the evening between North Carolina and Kansas. In a private room on the other side of the locker room, I had a video player and television set up—and one by one, I called the guys over to watch their videotapes again.

Bobby Hurley, Grant Hill, and Billy McCaffrey all watched their tapes. Then I called Christian Laettner.

"Christian, come over here, let's watch your tape," I said.

But Laettner stood up in front of the entire team and said, "Coach, I don't need the damned tape. I'm ready to play right now."

And some of the other guys said, "Yeah, right, let's go!"

Laettner knew exactly what he was doing. His statement was not meant for me. It was meant for the rest of the team. 175

That was one of the beautiful things about Christian Laettner. He did things like that—things that just can't be taught. His statement at that moment was much more impactful than anything I could have said. He was being a team leader, setting the stage for what was to come next. It was a hell of a thing.

Then, as the team was preparing to take the court for warmups, we saw on the television that Kansas had beaten North Carolina in the first semifinal game. All of a sudden, I noticed a collective sigh of relief in the locker room. Nothing was spoken, but it was clear to me that people were relieved that UNC had lost.

Holy mackerel, I thought, our guys might think it's okay to lose now that our crosstown rival is out of the tournament. I know they were thinking that at least now, if they lose, they wouldn't do any worse than UNC. At that point I was looking for any potential chink in our armor.

"Listen up, fellas," I said to them. "There may be some of us who might be thinking that now we've gone as far as Carolina, so it's okay to lose. Well, forget it. Get any such thought out of your head right now. It is not okay to lose. It is not okay. Remember, this is *our* time! Now let's go out there and win!"

As the game began, I believed it was very, very important for us to get off to a good start. I knew UNLV would try to intimidate us, so I asked all of the guys to come to Bobby Hurley's defense because I believed he would be their target. And I remember Hurley saying, "I don't need any help!"

Sure enough, they went after him with shoves and pushes and tough talk. But Bobby shoved and pushed right back. As a matter of fact, Hurley's demeanor during the entire game was remarkable. He had "the look" on his face. He made incredible behind-the-back passes. His ball handling under intense pressure was flawless. Bobby Hurley was the leader of our team that day—and he led with his daring heart.

And what a terrific game it was—back and forth all night long.

We jumped out to a 15–6 lead, but UNLV fought back to lead by two points at the half, 43–41. During the second half, I sensed that the Runnin' Rebels were feeling some pressure because they couldn't shake us. And that pressure resulted in the game becoming more physical. There were several incidents of shoving and tackling on both sides. There were also a couple of intentional fouls called—even a technical foul. But our guys would simply not back down as the lead changed hands seven straight times.

With two and a half minutes left in the game, UNLV was up by five points and were controlling the pace of play. At that point, it really looked like they were going to win the game.

As we were coming down the floor, I saw UNLV switch to a zone defense—which they called their "amoeba" defense. I was just about to call a play from the bench when Bobby Hurley, instinctively and confidently, took a long three-point shot and made it. It was as big a shot as anyone has ever hit for Duke. He didn't look over at me to see what I wanted him to do. He just took the initiative and did it. I was so proud of him at that moment. I get chill bumps on my arms just thinking about it.

Instantly the momentum of the game changed. Now, at 76–74, we were down by only two with 2:14 remaining on the clock. Our guys were fired up and the Runnin' Rebels were shaken up.

Duke's defense was so tough that the 45-second shot clock ran out and UNLV did not even get a shot off on the next time down the court. It was the first time all season that the

Runnin' Rebels had run out the shot clock. Then Brian Davis took a great pass from Grant Hill and tied up the score with a layup. After exchanging a couple of foul shots, we got the ball back with about 30 seconds left and the score tied at 77.

I signaled for our delay offense and yelled from the bench, "If you get something for the basket, then go to the basket." Thomas Hill saw an opening and took it to the hoop. He missed, but Laettner was right there for the rebound.

As Laett went up for the shot, he was fouled with 12.7 seconds left on the clock. UNLV immediately called a timeout and, as our players were coming over to take their seats on the bench, my mind flashed back to the end of that Arizona game two years before—when Christian Laettner was at the foul line to win the game. He missed his shot, but our team rallied around him and told him, "It's okay. We win and we lose *together*."

Now Laettner is in the same situation—only this time it's in the Final Four. This time it's for the right to play in the national championship game. And this time when I looked down the bench, I saw Christian Laettner smiling at me. And before I could say a word, he said: "I got 'em, Coach. I got 'em."

Forty-seven thousand people in the stands, millions more watching at home, tie score—and Laettner smiles and says, "I got 'em."

"Okay," I replied. "After Christian hits his shots, we're going to double-team their guard and keep the ball out of his hands. Remember about the defensive rebound—no fouls."

The teams went back on the court and Christian Laettner, smiling at the foul line, swished both shots to give us the lead.

We play defense. UNLV takes a last-second three-point desperation shot. The ball bounces off the backboard into Bobby

Hurley's hands. He throws the ball high into the air. Game over. Final score: Duke 79, UNLV 77.

And we're in the national championship game against Kansas.

After the game, Christian Laettner spoke to the media. "There were about thirty people in the whole world who thought we could win this game. The players, the coaches, and the people who work with the team. That was it!"

Christian was right. But the fact that, as a team, *we* felt we could win, was all that mattered.

Handling Success

It was midnight by the time we got back to our hotel. We were staying at the Holiday Inn near the Indianapolis Airport, which was filled by Duke fans, families, and friends. Thousands of people were waiting for us.

After getting off the bus, we could barely get into the lobby, let alone through it. It was crazy. It was madness. People with drinks in their hands were raising toasts to the team. Students were screaming. Parents were hugging their kids, patting them on the back, and crying. "Oh, Bobby!" "Oh, Billy!" "Thomas!" "Tony!" "How wonderful!" "I love you! I love you!"

Now, I'm usually the guy who talks about the importance of family, hugs, and close relationships. But I found myself saying, "No, no, no. Don't do this. We have another game to play. We still have to beat Kansas for the national championship." I mean I was really scared. We shouldn't have been celebrating. It had the potential to hurt us for the big game.

So I immediately started pushing the guys to get up to their rooms. "Let's go, guys. Let's go."

But when we got upstairs, parties were spilling out into the hallways. People were everywhere.

I was shaking my head as I finally made it to my suite. But when I walked in, I found my mother chugging beers with my wife. They had their arms locked together so that my mom controlled the chugging. It was quite a sight.

And I said to them: "No, this isn't the time to celebrate. The time is Monday night. This is too soon!"

And my mom paused for a moment and said, with a laugh: "Get out of here, Mike. Go to your room and watch your videotape. You have a job to do."

I also recall that the whole sports world was sizzling with Duke's victory over powerhouse UNLV. A lot of sportscasters were calling it the greatest upset in the history of sports.

Well, how do you handle success like that? In business, it would be like winning the biggest contract the company ever signed—and then having to turn right around and win the biggest contract that was possible to win. No company, no matter how good they are, is going to win that next job on reputation alone. They're going to have to go out and earn it. The upcoming game against Kansas was going to test everything I had taught the team that year, everything I believed in as a coach.

Next Game

We had put everything we had into that UNLV game—total focus, total concentration, all our energy, all our heart. Now we had to shake off UNLV and do it all over again for Kansas. We had to do it in less than forty-eight hours. And then we had to go out and beat another champion—because all the teams

who make it to the Final Four are champions. To put it suc-
cinctly, Kansas was another great, great team.

For me, preparation for the Kansas game began the moment the final buzzer sounded in the UNLV game. Everybody
was screaming and jumping around. But if you watch the
game on video, I can be seen walking out on the court mo-
tioning with my palms down for the team to settle down.
"Take it easy," I was saying. "Calm down. We've got another
game to play."

At that moment of ecstasy, I was thinking about the next
game. Why? Because that ecstasy could very well cause us to
lose the next game. It certainly wasn't going to help us on the
court against Kansas.

So I immediately put the game behind me. For me, the
UNLV victory was already in the past.

Just like in the regular season, our team has to put the last
game behind us quickly. Win or lose, we have to forget about
what happened yesterday and move on to tomorrow. During
the Final Four, you just have to speed up the process a little
bit.

After the UNLV game, after my mom sent me to my room,
our staff stayed up all night preparing for the Kansas game. We
studied videotapes, discussed options, outlined strategy. And
all the time, we could hear the partying going on outside in
the hall and in the next room.

When the sun finally came up, we showered, shaved, had
breakfast, and got on the team bus headed to the Hoosier
Dome for practice.

And I did not like what I saw.

The first thing I noticed was that two of our freshmen
were wearing Indiana Jones hats.

"What's going on?" I said to myself.

Other members of the team didn't have their warmup suits zipped up. They looked sloppy. I watched the players strut into the Hoosier Dome—it was a cocky, arrogant kind of walk. I studied their body language, their mannerisms, the way they talked to one another, the way they smirked. And I didn't like anything I saw—nothing.

So when we got into the locker room, I asked all the managers, trainers, and doctors to leave. "Everybody out except the players and coaches," I said sternly.

And then I blistered them.

"I don't like the way you look. I don't like the way you walk. I don't like the way you talk. I don't like the way you dress. You guys are still living the UNLV game. You should just go back to the hotel and let everyone kiss your rear and pat you on the back. You should just go watch the tape of the UNLV game because there's no way in hell you can beat a great team like Kansas. No way. Only an ordinary team would be satisfied beating UNLV. But an ordinary team won't win tomorrow night—because an ordinary team cannot beat a great team. Now get the hell out of here."

And I stormed out of the locker room into a side office.

Five minutes later, I came out to see if my tirade had done any good. But nobody was in the locker room.

As I walked out into the eerily quiet arena, I saw a sight I will never, ever forget. To this day, it gives me chills.

All the players had gathered together at center court. They were just standing there waiting for me.

But there was something about the *way* they were standing.

Their faces. The looks in their eyes. The fact that they were close together. They were standing as a team. They were telling me they were ready. And they didn't have to say a damn word.

At that moment I knew we were going to win the national championship. I knew then and there that they had cleansed themselves of a big victory and opened themselves to the opportunity for an even bigger victory.

The final score of the Kansas game was 72–65.

Duke University won its first national championship.

And after the game my mom came up to me and said: "*Mike!* You *see!* I *told* you you'd do better this year!"

COACH K's TIPS

- When events beyond your control pull you away from your team, delegate as much as possible.

- Don't forget that each individual on your team needs to take responsibility for their own performance.

- A leader's job is to remove any obstacle that can negatively impact his team's performance.

- During critical periods, a leader is not allowed to feel sorry for himself, to be down, to be angry, or to be weak. Leaders must beat back these emotions.

- In order to beat an overwhelming adversary, it takes unbelievable focus and concentration.

- During critical moments, look closely for any potential chink in your armor. And then take action to fix it.

- Encourage members of your team to take the initiative and act on their own.

- No organization, no matter how good it is, is going to win on reputation alone.

- A moment of ecstasy might very well cause you to lose the next game. Put it behind you and move on.

- When you cleanse yourself of a big victory, you may open yourself up to the opportunity for an even bigger victory.

12

CELEBRATE TRADITION

"People want to be on a team. They want to be part of something bigger than themselves. They want to be in a situation where they feel that they are doing something for the greater good."

—**Coach K**

"The Cameron Crazies are our sixth man. They're part of our team. When they root for us, it's not the fans rooting for the team, it's the team rooting for the team."

—**Coach K**

"We try to create a legacy that binds the past to the present."

—**Coach K**

After the last game of the season, win or lose, I will thank our team.

"I loved coaching you guys," I'll say in the locker room. And then I'll go around to each of the players individually, shake their hands, give them a hug, and say a heartfelt and sincere "Thank you."

I do that with every team every year. It's a personal tradition. And even though the last game has been played, the season isn't over until we hold our annual awards banquet at Cameron Indoor Stadium.

Every year, a thousand or more people show up for the banquet—players, coaches, managers, trainers, staff members—everyone associated with that year's Duke basketball team plus their families. It's an unbelievably festive mood partly because it's like a big family gathering. We give out a variety of individual and team awards, which are often presented by members of past Duke basketball teams. And we also put on a show—a really fun show.

I want the team to feel good about what they've done that year—what they've achieved. I also want to give them a chance to celebrate the journey they experienced. We couldn't celebrate during the season because we always had to move on to the next game. There was never really a chance to savor our successes.

So we put together a composite videotape with highlights of the year. Set to music, the video tells a story. In essence, it relives the journey, and it reinforces that it was a good journey—wherever it may have taken us.

The banquet is a time for everyone associated with the team. They worked hard all year—sometimes without a pat on the back, sometimes without adequate appreciation—but always with dedication, pride, and determination. They deserve to have a night all their own. They deserve to be treated with honor.

I often think about the guys who fought in Vietnam who came home to no parades, no celebrations, no thank-yous. And I am determined that the same thing will never happen to any team of mine after it completes a long journey. This annual awards banquet gives us the chance to do all that for our team and more.

It also gives us the opportunity to honor our departing seniors. They've been on a four-*year* journey with Duke. So we produce a separate video for each senior that relives their entire time with us. Mickie labors for weeks choosing video clips and editing them so that each film will mean something special. And she also chooses one special song for each senior that is played as the story runs. Each short video is a work of art—and a labor of love.

187

Before his video is shown, the senior gets a chance to get up and express his personal feelings to everyone about his Duke experience. He can say what he wants to say. It's his night. And then he receives a personal copy of his video. It's a gift from the Krzyzewski family. No matter what the kid has done in his four years—whether he was an All-America or didn't play that much—I want him to leave knowing that he was part of our family, will always be part of our family, and we thank him for it.

A Part of Something Bigger

We instituted this form of awards banquet, with a family-type atmosphere, honoring the seniors, videos of the journey, and so on, not long after I arrived at Duke. At first, it was deemed by others to be "an interesting idea." Now, of course, after nearly two decades, it is an established tradition.

We patterned it, in part, after the graduation parade at West Point. At the end of every year, the corps of cadets come out onto the reviewing field. The graduating seniors separate, march straight ahead, and then turn around and face the rest of the cadets. And then the corps passes in review of the senior class.

As much as I didn't like parades when I was at West Point, honoring the seniors in such a symbolic manner was touching to me. Of course, when I was a plebe, I was glad to see those clowns go—as hard as they were on us. But as I progressed, I began to appreciate it more and more. And when I was a senior, myself, I appreciated it the most—and I will never forget the feeling I had on the day of the graduation parade when the rest of the cadets passed by us.

I saw the corps *without* me. But then I realized that the corps would *never* be without me. I would always be a part of West Point. Once a member of the corps, always a member of the corps.

And that's the way I want it to be for everyone who has participated in Duke basketball: once a part of Duke, always a part of Duke.

Tradition helps make that a reality.

It also helps motivate people. It makes them *want* to come back. They *desire* to go on another journey. Tradition builds pride, fosters team unity, and reinforces confidence. It lets people know that they are part of something grand.

And I find that people, generally, want to be on a team. They want to be part of something bigger than themselves. They want to be in a situation where they feel that they are doing something for the greater good.

Therefore, if people really are part of something with a lot of tradition, they will be less likely to be jealous of a teammate or do something detrimental to the organization. For example, I would never do anything to harm West Point. Grant Hill would never do anything to harm Duke.

In essence, tradition makes it more difficult to bring out the negative aspects of human nature. "Hey, I better be careful. I have to live up to the legacy of Grant Hill and Johnny Dawkins and Tommy Amaker and Mark Alarie." That's a powerful form of motivation for any leader.

Another simple fact that motivates players is the standard of excellence that the organization has already established. People are proud to be part of a top-notch group. And Duke's basketball program is renowned for producing a winning team year after year—and making it to the Final Four more often than any other school in the last twenty years. That kind of consistency, especially in postseason play, engenders pride. Even people outside the basketball program become more prominent because of their association with Duke University.

And I've found that most don't take it for granted. Our fans, our alumni, our faculty, our students, our associates all realize that it takes hard work to achieve what we do year in and year out. I don't think they would be disappointed just because we didn't get to the Final Four. They might be disappointed if they ever felt we didn't make the effort to get there. But we do not need to win a national championship to verify what Duke stands for today—nor legitimize the great things Duke has achieved in the past.

Binding the Past to the Present

You know, there is something about Yankee pinstripes. There is something about the marine corps dress uniform. And there is something about a Duke basketball jersey.

When our freshmen put one on for the first time, they know they should be proud of it, but they may not know exactly why. Well, over the next four years, we teach them why.

People with names like Dawkins, Gminski, Groat, Hill, Hurley, Ferry, Laettner, and Mullins all wore that jersey. And tens of thousands of students attended and graduated from Duke University who are used to seeing that jersey, who have pride in those four letters: D-U-K-E.

That's why even if, once in a while, the overall design of the uniform changes—like larger shorts or a slight color adjustment—the block letters that spell Duke never change. Never.

Putting on a Duke uniform means something in our program. Just seeing it engenders pride. It raises emotions and it brings back memories. It binds the past to the present and, therefore, symbolizes Duke tradition.

Cameron Indoor Stadium, where we play all our home games, does the same. Cameron is not a large 40,000-seat coliseum. Rather, it is a refurbished, un-air-conditioned, old-fashioned campus gym with beautiful interior woodwork and a personality all its own. Championship banners hang from the rafters along with retired numbers of a select few players. In 1999, *Sports Illustrated* ranked Cameron Indoor Stadium as the number four active venue for sports in the twentieth century—along with places like Wrigley Field and Yankee Stadium.

Small, close, and intimate, Cameron provides a great view of the game no matter where a fan may be sitting. On the lower level, students surround the court on all four sides. The rest of our fans sit up in the second level. The school pep band adds to an atmosphere that is both exhilarating for the home team and intimidating for a visiting team.

Duke teams have been playing and winning basketball games for more than half a century at Cameron Indoor Stadium. Over the years, there have been suggestions to build a new, modern arena. But I politely decline the thought. Even though people are well intentioned, Cameron is a tradition that can never be rebuilt once it's gone. It has to be looked after, cared for, and nurtured just like the rest of our family.

The last game we play in Cameron every year, our final home contest of the season, is also a very special day for our organization. We call it "Senior Day" in honor of the members of our team who will be playing their last game in front of our students and fans and under the banners and lights of our very special indoor arena.

We actually begin Senior Day the night before when 191

Mickie, my daughters, and I have a private dinner with the graduating seniors. Another personal tradition I have is to pull them aside just before game time for a moment alone. I make it a point to tell them how much I care about them and how much they've meant to our program. "I love you guys. You've been great. Let's go out and make this one of our best."

Just prior to tip-off, the seniors are introduced separately and they stand in the center jump circle all alone to acknowledge the cheers and appreciation of the fans. And after the game is played, win or lose, the seniors go back out on the court to say goodbye to their classmates.

As the students come out of their seats and crowd around the players, each senior takes a turn at the microphone to say thank you for all the support, all the love, all the caring, all those years. It's a very emotional moment—and it is just for the students.

I usually position myself in a back corner out of sight. I don't want to take any attention away from their moment, but I also want to listen in. And I don't think there is a single time in twenty years that I've listened in where I didn't have tears in my eyes by the time it was over.

The Sixth Man

It's easy to see the members of our team who are on the court all the time—and by that I mean the players, of course. It's not so easy to recognize all of the other people who contribute to the success of our organization—people out in the community, fans, supporters, students.

Our staff, players, assistant coaches all work very hard to cultivate relationships with all these people. In the fall of each year, we'll set up meetings with fraternities, sororities, and other groups on campus. One or two of our players may accompany the coach to these meetings, where attendance usually ranges from forty to 100. The coach may show a highlight tape and then make a short presentation followed by a question-and-answer period.

I also will participate in several luncheons sponsored by the Duke University Student Union. These gatherings are a great opportunity for me to promote interaction between the students and our basketball program. And I really enjoy the time spent just sitting and chatting with the young people. I think they enjoy it, too. And I also believe it makes them feel more appreciated, more a part of our team.

In truth, the students *are* part of our team. They are our sixth man.

When they arrive at the games, many have painted their faces, designed humorous signs, created chants that echo throughout the arena during a game. They call themselves the Cameron Crazies.

They sit at floor level—like the players on the bench. But they very rarely actually sit. They stand when the team stands. When the team comes out on the court for warmups, the Cameron Crazies are standing. While there's action during the game, they're standing. They only sit when the team sits—at halftime or timeouts.

Most people in the stands cheer in reaction to a play. But the sixth man cheers because they feel they can help make a play. Actually, they can and do often have a major influence during a game. With all their cheering and all the noise they generate, they can make something happen. And when something good happens, they don't cheer so much because they're entertained, they cheer for the same reason the players on the bench cheer—because one of their teammates has just scored.

I remember once being asked in an interview what I thought about the Cameron Crazies as fans rooting for our team. "Well," I replied, "the Cameron Crazies are our sixth man. They're part of our team. When they root for us, it's not the fans rooting for the team, it's the team rooting for the team."

All our home games are sellouts. Every single one. And tickets are always first-come, first-serve for the students. So in order to get the best seats, they camp out.

At times, part of the perimeter outside Cameron Indoor Stadium is lined with up to 100 or more tents where 1,500 to 2,000 students take turns holding positions in line. And the kids make the most of it. They hang out, party, huddle around fires set in garbage cans, and generally have a great time, sometimes camping out for a couple of weeks depending on who the upcoming opponent is.

The students have named this tent village "Krzyzewskiville." And I love it. I love the enthusiasm. Sometimes, I'll send over pizza and soft drinks to the kids in the tents, or pass out T-shirts—or I'll just walk out and say hi to them.

Before our home game with North Carolina, I will bring all the kids from Krzyzewskiville into Cameron for a big team meeting. During my talk, I try to enlighten them as to how they might better support us in the game.

If there are any problems, this is the time to address them. For instance, once or twice in the past, there have been some incidents of students throwing tennis balls across the court to other sections of the bleachers—or trying to harass opposing players during pregame introductions. I always advise the students to cheer *for* Duke, not *against* our opponents. "I really do not think we need to be abusive," I'll tell them. "Be positive. Remember, you are our sixth man—a part of our team. So you should act responsibly."

During this meeting—and don't forget that there are sometimes several thousand Cameron Crazies who show up— I also take time to personally thank the students for the support they have given us. One year, I recall, there were some rumors going around about naming a building after me and I quietly asked that the suggestion be dropped.

"People talk about naming this building and that building after me," I said to the kids in the stadium that year, "but I don't really care about any of that. What I do hope for is that there will always be a Krzyzewskiville. That's what I want my name on. I'm proud of it because it was named by you kids and because it is living. A building is not living, but Krzyzewskiville is. It is alive because of all of you. I'm proud that you honored me in such a way."

During this gathering with the students, I will often discuss the scouting report and the battle plan for the upcoming game. Occasionally, I will ask the sixth man to help us by giving them a specific assignment. And I have never asked the students at Duke for something that they didn't give me. They've always been terrific. One year, I told them that one of our defensive goals for the game would be to force the ball along the sidelines, and that whenever our opponents picked up their dribble in those situations, I wanted our players to yell, "Ball! Ball!"

Well, the next day, before the game actually started, I walked out onto the court to say hello to small groups of students who were waiting in their seats—and we briefly discussed what their assignment was again. And sure enough, during the game, we forced a few of those situations and it wasn't just the players on the court who were yelling, "Ball! Ball!" It was the entire student body. We won that game, and as I walked off the court, I pointed to the students and kept mouthing the words, "*You* did this. *You* did this."

The NCAA has a rule that, at the beginning of every year, practice may begin on a certain date. On that day, at 12:01 A.M., you can have your first practice. In 1997, we had just completed that "Midnight Madness" practice in front of a capacity crowd and I had lined up all our players in the center of the court for a team picture. The cameraman was getting positioned in the rafters for a unique, down-facing shot, when I looked up and called for everyone's attention.

"Wait a minute. Wait a minute. Something's wrong with this picture. Somebody's missing. It's our sixth man. All of you in the stands, come down here on the court and get in this shot."

So several thousand students came out of the stands and, with respect and dignity, quietly lined up. They looked at it as an honor to be included.

On the walls of our locker room, we have placed framed pictures of our players in various poses—making a shot, grabbing a rebound, or standing on the sidelines. So we hung that 1997–1998 team picture alongside all the others. It was our way of telling the sixth man that they are part of our team— and that *we* are part of *their* team.

That's the way I want it to be at Duke University. We don't have an elite group of basketball players playing for the rest of the students. We have students, who happen to be basketball players, representing the rest of the student body at Duke University.

That's what college basketball should be all about. That kind of philosophy not only preserves the purity of the game, it reminds everyone that the paramount goal is to secure an outstanding college education. That's the best tradition of all.

At Duke, we strive for consistency on the court, vying for league championships, going to the NCAA tournament, going to the Final Four, maybe winning a championship—all while still producing a college graduate.

A tradition like that is huge if you can develop it. And you have to work year in and year out to do it. But all the hard work is worth it, because once you make it happen, confidence, excellence, unity, and pride will grow.

Great tradition is like the moisture that prepares the soil. It helps the ground absorb more water, become more fertile, and it allows important things to grow to their fullest capabilities. That's what I want for all the kids who play basketball for me. I want them to grow into men of strong character, men who are leaders themselves.

I also want all my guys to love having played at Duke University. On the last game of the season, which is usually a loss in tournament play, I don't want them to think of their careers as having ended on a loss. I want them to think of the great journey we had—of our mistakes and successes, of our peaks and our valleys, of our hopes and our dreams.

And I want them to have enjoyed our association with one another. I want every journey to conclude the way it did for Tommy Amaker.

After we lost in the Sweet Sixteen of the NCAA tournament during his senior year, Tommy and I hugged each other and cried like little boys. And it wasn't because we had lost a basketball game. It was because we both knew, at that moment, that we were at the end of our personal journey together, as player and coach.

I want each player who plays for Duke to know that our relationship will always be there—that friends do not disappear once the journey has concluded.

Friendship is a matter of the heart.

And all my friends remain in my heart, forever.

Coach K's Tips

- At the end of every season, thank your team for their effort.
- Give your team a chance to celebrate the journey they experienced. Make it fun for them. They deserve to have a night all their own.
- With enough time, an interesting idea can become an established tradition.
- Tradition helps motivate people. It makes them want to come back. They desire to go on another journey.
- If people are part of something with a lot of tradition, they will be less likely to be jealous of a teammate or do something detrimental to the organization.
- Tradition makes it more difficult to bring out the negative aspects of human nature.
- Consistent excellence engenders pride.
- Honor the seniors in your organization.
- Cultivate relationships with people who support your organization.
- Once tradition is in place, confidence, excellence, unity, and pride will grow.

ALL-SEASON

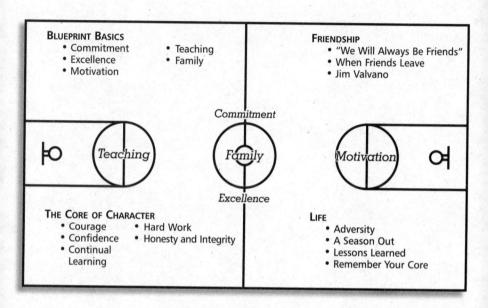

BLUEPRINT BASICS
- Commitment
- Excellence
- Motivation
- Teaching
- Family

FRIENDSHIP
- "We Will Always Be Friends"
- When Friends Leave
- Jim Valvano

Commitment

Teaching

Family

Motivation

Excellence

THE CORE OF CHARACTER
- Courage
- Confidence
- Continual Learning
- Hard Work
- Honesty and Integrity

LIFE
- Adversity
- A Season Out
- Lessons Learned
- Remember Your Core

"Early in our marriage, when Mike was the head basketball coach at West Point, I told him that one day I was going to write a book and I already had the title: The Season Never Ends.*"*

—MICKIE KRZYZEWSKI

13

BLUEPRINT BASICS

"It's important to remember that every person is different and has to be motivated differently."

—Coach K

"When our goal is to try to do our best, when our focus is on preparation and sacrifice and effort—instead of numbers on the scoreboard—we will never lose."

—Coach K

"I'm a teacher and a coach."

—Coach K

A couple of days after we won our first national championship, in April 1991, Christian Laettner came into my office and plopped himself down on the couch.

"Coach," he said, "I'm really tired. I mean I'm beat."

"Well, I can understand that," I replied. "You should be tired. You had an unbelievable year."

"They want me to participate in the trials for the Pan American Games. But I don't want to do it. I want to rest."

"Look, Christian," I said softly, "the Pan Am Games can be really important for a couple of reasons. First, let me talk about how it's important for the team.

"For us to win our second national championship, you have to get better. You're the leader of the team. You have to show your teammates that you want to improve and that you still have the commitment to not take time off until the end of next season. That would provide an unbelievable example as the leader of our basketball team."

"You mean I shouldn't take any break?" Christian asked.

"No, not at all. Let's think about doing this: Let's call USA Basketball and ask for a waiver so that you don't have to participate in the trials. We'll just tell them that you need some rest, which you do. They know you're going to make the team. We all know you're going to make the team. Don't touch a basketball for the next six weeks. Just get away from the game. Be a college student. Relax. Have some fun. Rest up. Then, a couple of weeks before the Pan Am team begins practice, you can start working out."

"That sounds pretty good," he said.

"Then do the Pan American Games. After that, take another month off. I won't include you in our preseason program. So you'll get most of the summer off, you'll rest up, but you'll still participate in the Pan Am Games. That will really help the team and it will show great leadership."

"Okay, I like it."

"It's also good for you personally, Christian. Why is it good for you?" I asked him.

"Well, I get to represent my country."

"Right, that's really important. But there's one more reason. Next summer, there's going to be one or two college players picked for the Olympics. I think we are going to have a chance to win the national championship again. You are going to have a chance to be named Player of the Year. By then, you will also have played not only in the Goodwill Games, but in the Pan American Games, and the World Championships. Overall, I think you will have a great opportunity to make the United States Olympic basketball team."

"Coach, that sounds great. Let's do it."

"Okay. Now get outta here and get some rest."

Commitment

That summer, Christian Laettner did everything I advised him to do. And the following year, we *did* win the national championship, he *was* named Player of the Year, and he *did* make the Olympic team. As a matter of fact, Christian was the only college player selected on the gold-medal-winning Dream Team—the first year professional athletes were allowed to compete in the Olympics.

In that situation, I think both Christian Laettner and I demonstrated a great deal of commitment to each other and to the team. I would not have been doing either him or our team any favors if I had agreed with him that he should take the entire summer off. Nor would it have helped matters if I had demanded that he play in the Pan Am Games or if I had tried to make him feel guilty by saying something like: "How could you not do that for your country?"

Instead, I made suggestions and guided him to make the right decision. I knew that Christian was tired and that if he made a decision on his own at that moment, he was likely to make the wrong decision. I also thought he'd probably regret not playing in the Pan Am Games once he was finally rested.

My early commitment to him and his parents was to give 100 percent of myself in coaching, teaching, and advising whatever was in his best interests. Going to the Pan Am Games helped him grow as a player and as a person. He became a better leader for our team—and the level of his play rose significantly as a result.

Personally, and as the head coach, I would have regretted a wrong decision. It was the right thing to do for our basketball team. If Christian showed his commitment at that point, the way we structured it together, everyone else on the team would have an easier time being committed. In other words, if the leader is committed, there will be a greater chance for the followers to be committed.

Laettner was the leader on the team. Everything revolved around him. All the other players knew he was tired. His actions set the tone and inspired the rest of the team to commit themselves to try to win the national championship again. Laettner showed everybody that he was still hungry, that he wanted to have another great year. To me, that is a major form of commitment.

A leader has to let his players have the freedom to show their personal commitment to the organization. If people invest time in something, they are more likely to become valued members of the organization. So I utilize the summers as a time to give the players a chance to demonstrate their personal commitment.

In general, the summer is a great time for a player to learn more about himself. If he constantly stays in the role that is expected of him, there is a great tendency that he will be confined to that role. He begins to accept a certain set of limitations for his performance. But, given the opportunity, he may be capable of much more.

So we encourage our players to keep active, to do different things during the summer that help them develop and grow as people. And it does not necessarily have to be something in basketball—like the Pan Am Games or the Goodwill Games. Shane Battier, for instance, spent one summer working as a stock analyst on Wall Street. He spent another summer in Chicago working for a big marketing firm. Other players do similar things. And then they come back to us in August or early September with new skills and a greater maturity. In turn, that helps the *team's* overall skill and maturity.

It's similar to many large companies who have offices in different cities around the country. It's not a bad idea to have an accountant or an engineer visit those offices for a few weeks. It gives them a chance to learn more about various aspects of the overall organization. And it exposes them to other skill sets. It's like sending them to an executive program to prepare them for a future higher leadership role in the company. If they are going to progress up the line, they will need to be exposed to the intricacies of all the various aspects of the organization.

A leader must be committed to helping people grow. My commitment to each player is to help him realize his full potential, to be the best he can be. And his commitment to me is to try to do his best. Overall, we strive for a commitment to our organization, a commitment to our team, and a commitment to one another. And there is always a commitment to excellence.

Excellence

Every now and then, I will talk to our players about the Duke Chapel and the beautiful wood carvings on the altar—which all of them have seen.

"Fellas, remember all the magnificent, intricate detail in the woodwork on that altar?" I'll say. "The person who did that work was an artist in every sense of the word."

"Who did the artist do that for?" I'll ask them.

"Well, he was paid by somebody."

"Probably. But I believe the artist who did this work would take the same care and be just as precise if he were whittling on a stick next to a stream. He would do it because he wants to please himself, because he takes pride in everything he does, and because a true artist is about excellence.

"Well, fellas, that's what we should want to do. We should want to be excellent in everything we do—and we should want to please ourselves. Then, hopefully, people will look at our work on the court and say the same thing we're saying about that altar: 'Hey, that's pretty damn good.'

"An artist has his own expectation levels and sets his own standards. And whether he's getting paid one dollar or one million dollars, he's going to do the same great job. He's going to put everything he has into it—every time out. That's excellence. That's pride."

My personal motivation as a coach has always been the pursuit of excellence. I'd rather create a masterpiece every time out than have peaks and valleys where I'm superb one day and mediocre the next. In addition, I do not let someone else define excellence for me. I feel good about what I'm doing just because I'm doing it.

When a leader is constantly in the public eye, it's tempting to let the media determine whether his team is as great or as bad as they are made out to be. It's like that sculptor or a painter, who has to block out what other people say about his work. You may get some good suggestions. But, ultimately, you have to paint for yourself.

My hunger is not for success, it is for excellence. Because when you attain excellence, success just naturally follows.

Motivation

Right after we won our first NCAA tournament—around the same time I had that long conversation with Christian

Laettner about the Pan Am Games—the media began talking about Duke "defending the national championship."

Well, I immediately called our group together.

"I don't want anybody on this team to allow the press to set our goals for us or to define our dreams for us," I said to the players as we were all gathered in the locker room. "We are not *defending* a national championship. The word 'defending' implies that we will be back on our heels protecting something. No way, guys. We cannot win another national championship on our reputation. We have to go out and earn everything we get. We are not *defending* anything. We are *pursuing* a national championship. *Pursuing!*"

I did not have to think too long about calling the players together for that little motivation session. I felt it was important, so I took action immediately. A leader cannot motivate people by simply writing something down on paper, handing it out, and then saying, "Here, do this!" You've got to know people. You've got to do different things in different situations. And that makes every day different from the day before.

My goal for each player, and for the team as a whole, is to have them playing in a positive matter, utilizing their abilities, and not being afraid to fail. That's my goal in motivation. If a leader can get everyone in his organization doing that, he's going to be in pretty good shape.

But motivation also has to be looked at both individually and as a team effort. Most players have a certain degree of self-motivation or they wouldn't be playing in the first place. It's the leader's challenge to motivate each player in such a way that he performs at his best while helping the team perform at its best.

So how does a leader achieve that kind of motivation?

Well, I don't know why, but I've always seemed to have

something of a natural knack for motivating people. My buddy from Chicago, Moe Mlynski, once told a reporter that when we were growing up together, people wanted to be on my team "because you knew he would win," as Moe phrased it. "He knew how to get you to play better, even in high school. I look back now and see his ability even then. He's got a special gift."

I think I just naturally key in on human nature. I look at how people react to different things—as individuals and as a group. A leader has to get into a person's head—and then know what button to push at any given moment.

In general, my style is to be flexible and versatile. In other words, I think there's a time to get in someone's face and there's a time when you just put it on the line without yelling. There's also a time when you pat on the back. And there's a time when you hug.

The only way to know when to do what is to look at each situation differently. Each moment requires its own maneuver.

In that same vein, it's also important to remember that every person is different and has to be motivated differently. One player might respond to a pat on the rear, another might need to be kicked in the rear. And still another might need no attention at all. Some people respond when you challenge them, others when you encourage them. Some people respond when criticized. And some go into a shell with even the slightest bit of criticism.

The leader of the team is responsible for getting to know the players well enough to understand what methods are the most effective for each individual—as well as the team as a whole. And so we're back to relationships and communication again.

I once heard a high school coach tell a kid that it was not

his job to motivate players, that they should show up motivated. Well, I just shook my head. I could not disagree more with a statement like that. I believe the main job of a coach is to motivate. The main job of a leader is to inspire.

Inspiration and motivation are ongoing concerns. Throughout the course of the year, I give my players motivational reading material at least a couple of times each month. Sometimes it is an article and other times it may be just an inspirational quote or two. I also try to motivate our players in all aspects of their lives throughout the whole year. I write to the guys over the summer and I call them to discuss how they are progressing. Certainly, I want our players motivated to perform at high levels during the season, but I also must remember that they may need some encouragement in the summer with their workout and conditioning programs—or with their academics.

A person, or a team, can work hard to be successful. And once success is achieved, it's very easy to sit back and think that success will just come again—like rain on the rooftops. But I've found that it is much harder to stay on top than it is to get there.

To stay successful, you have to stay hungry. A leader should not allow his team to cheat themselves with complacency.

Teaching

I'm a teacher and a coach. I surround myself with other good teachers on my staff. And our whole approach to coaching revolves around teaching. To be considered a good basketball coach, you must be able to teach the game. And make no mistake about it, teaching is an art.

Successful teaching can be accomplished in many different ways, but planning what you teach is of the utmost importance. A coach may have plenty of basketball knowledge, but his teaching ability will be judged by what his players know and what they are able to achieve under game conditions. In my opinion, the most important aspect of teaching is being able to translate your knowledge to enhance performance of your team.

Can your players become instinctive in their gamelike habits and react as one when they are playing offense or defense? A positive answer to that question is my goal when I teach my basketball team each season.

Every summer, we have about 1,200 youngsters in town for our Duke Basketball Camp. Mickie and my daughters all work at the camp and it's always sold out.

Now, I can get tired of traveling—but I never get tired of the camp. It excites me, partly because of the enthusiasm of all the kids, and partly because teaching is what I love most in the world.

Teaching, of course, is the most important part of our camp. Our emphasis is on fundamentals based on the age and skill level of each camper. When a camper leaves Duke, we hope he has had a good time and has shown improvement. We also hope that in some way we have helped him become a better person.

The players on our Duke basketball team, if they wish, also have an opportunity to participate as teachers. I really believe it helps our players' development to get involved with the camp. When they teach young kids the fundamentals of basketball, they are also reminding themselves about what they, themselves, should always be doing. They're saying, they're showing, they're doing—all with younger people. In essence, they are learning themselves. And to teach is to learn twice, as the adage goes.

Once our regular season begins again, I find that the players who participated in the camp are easier to teach—which is a side benefit to me. That's another reason I encourage our players to go and play on other teams for other coaches. When they participate in international competition, I know they will have the opportunity to learn some new things from the great coaching staffs that are assembled.

A leader can't be afraid to let someone else educate members of his team. They can only obtain a broader perspective by venturing out on their own. Also, when I get them back after the summer, I invariably have found that they've grown—both in the knowledge of their sport and in their development as people. I also find that, upon their return, the players have often obtained a greater appreciation for what they have at Duke.

"Man, am I ever glad I'm playing for you," I've heard from more than one returning player.

"Boy, Coach, I really like the way we travel better."

And when they get back, I'll ask them if they picked up anything that our Duke team might be able to utilize.

"What did you like about the way they did it?" I'll ask. "I mean, be honest."

"Well, I really liked this neat little drill they did in practice."

"Show it to me. Maybe we can use it."

While we are teaching our players, we can also learn from them. If you're a good teacher, you know that the arrow goes both ways. You give to the group. The group gives back to you.

I think it takes tremendous confidence to be able to send

your kids off to learn from another coach and then come back to your system. Some leaders, especially in competitive businesses, feel that an outstanding employee might be hired away by an outside firm. And that's a valid concern. But if you really have a strong relationship with the individual, and you've treated him right in the past, it's a risk worth taking—especially when you consider the potential knowledge and experience he might bring back to your organization.

I have been associated with sports all of my life, as a player and as a coach. I have learned more about myself and others through sports than through any other avenue. And I'm still learning, both from the situations I encounter and the youngsters I teach.

One of the things I have learned, and will always believe, is that participation in college sports is a vital part of education at the highest level. It affords young men and women throughout the country the opportunity to learn about themselves and to share their experiences. What better place to learn about trust, teamwork, integrity, friendship, commitment, collective responsibility, and so many other values than in college sports?

Where better to learn about handling success and failure?

Where better to learn to work with other people to overcome the obstacles that can prevent all of us from reaching our true potential?

Where better to learn to express enthusiasm appropriately, to develop discipline, and to polish communication skills?

I believe that college sports, as an extension of what we do and learn in the classroom, is an invaluable part of higher education.

And for me personally, the best thing about my profession

is that I can teach. The personal relationships that are developed, the impact that I'm able to have on the young people in their development as human beings, is incredibly worthwhile to me.

Teaching is the heart of my coaching style. If I teach them well, winning games will be the natural result. If my goal had to be only winning games, I wouldn't be a coach.

Trying to do your best, learning about your limits, and then trying to extend them—this is the proper perspective for a leader to have. As teachers and coaches, we should remember that when mere winning is our only goal, we are doomed to disappointment and failure. But when our goal is to try to do our best, when our focus is on preparation and sacrifice and effort—instead of on numbers on the scoreboard—we will never lose.

Family

When I was growing up, I was proud to be a member of the Krzyzewski family. It was the strongest single group I've ever been associated with. And, now, I live every day of my life being proud of my family and where I came from. What price can a person pay for that?

Because my family has made me stronger and better, it seems like a natural thing to run our team like a family. So from the very beginning, we tell our players that they are not only members of a basketball team, they are joining a basketball family.

There are a lot of commonsense advantages to running a team like a family—honesty, strength, caring, and so on. But one of the greatest strengths is the fact that, in a family, you are never alone. There are built-in allies.

Being part of a strong family makes a person achieve more, because the accomplishment can be shared. And it creates a built-in form of support when things go wrong. When you achieve something, there's a party with other members of the family. When you experience a loss, there's crying and sharing.

If there's a setback, someone comes to your rescue. In essence, a family makes you strong enough to take a few hits. You can't be knocked out with one punch. In other words, if you're part of a strong family, your heart cannot be broken as easily by any single opponent. And that's worth a great deal to any coach.

When I was growing up, I was never afraid to fail. I always felt that if I had to jump out of a burning building, there would be a safety net waiting for me. And that safety net was my family. That is what I want for our players.

I always knew my mother, my father, and my brother would be there for me. I knew because they loved me. And, as a basketball coach, I have no problem telling a team, "I love you guys."

When I say that, there's absolutely nothing phony about it. The feeling of love develops as we move through the process. How we greet each other, often going from a handshake to a hug, is something that just happens between me and a member of the team—and among members of the team with one another.

I try to convey the idea to all members of our team that we are not just playing basketball. I would hope that our kids would see that we love them. I would hope that the players who played here in the past would say that they loved playing

217

at Duke; that they loved a teammate; that they loved the situation they were in.

Sharing with one another and caring for one another—that's what love is. That's what family is all about.

Family is a fist—complete with communication, caring, trust, pride, and collective responsibility. Family makes individuals part of something bigger.

If leaders can achieve the feeling of family in their organizations, success will be just around the corner.

My wife and daughters Debbie and Jamie traveled with me to the Final Four in Charlotte in 1994, where our first opponent was to be the University of Florida. Our daughter Lindy was due to arrive the afternoon of that game.

But the day before, as she was in the parking lot of a local shopping center in Durham, a man with a gun tried to force his way into her car. She somehow managed to get away and run off through the parking lot while the man drove away with her car.

After we found out she was not hurt, we asked a friend to immediately bring her to Charlotte. When she arrived, we not only hugged and kissed her, we bombarded her with questions. "I just kept thinking he was going to shoot me in the back," I remember her saying. What a nightmare that thought is for any parent.

After a while, Lindy started tiring of all our questions. Even though a bit irritated, she kept answering when Mickie asked her what the man with the gun was wearing.

"He was wearing jeans and a black shirt. He had on a black belt and baseball cap."

"What was on the baseball cap?" Mickie asked.

Obviously frustrated with that last question, and wanting

the family focus to be on the task at hand, Lindy took a deep breath, turned to look me in the eye, and said: "Florida!"

My daughter was not only telling me that she was all right, she was telling me that we had to get on to the next thing. We had to win the first round of the Final Four. And the next night, we did defeat Florida in that game, which, in turn, allowed us to advance to the national championship game.

COACH K'S TIPS

- If the leader is committed, there will be a greater chance for the followers to be committed.

- Give your players the freedom to show their personal commitment to the organization.

- Hunger not for success, but for excellence. And don't let anyone else define excellence for you.

- Motivation has to be looked at both individually and as a team effort.

- Each moment requires its own maneuver.

- To stay successful, you have to stay hungry. Don't cheat yourself with complacency.

- Plan what you teach.

- While you're teaching your players, you can also learn from them.

- When your organization operates like a strong family, you can't be knocked out by one punch.

- Family is a fist—complete with communication, caring, trust, pride, and collective responsibility. Family makes individuals part of something bigger.

14

THE CORE OF CHARACTER

"Courage gives a leader the ability to stand straight and not sway no matter which way the wind blows."

—**Coach K**

"With accomplishment comes confidence and with confidence comes belief. It has to be in that order."

—**Coach K**

"Coach K will always tell you the truth."

—**Steve Wojciechowski (1995–1998)**

*I*n 1983, at the end of my third year as head basketball coach at Duke, I found myself sitting in a Denny's restaurant at 3:00 A.M. with my staff and a few friends. We were tucked away in a back corner of the place just staring at one another.

Earlier that evening, we had lost in the Atlantic Coast Conference tournament to Virginia by a score of 109–66—and we were down. That blowout ended our season with an 11-17 won-lost record, the second worst in Duke basketball history. We had set the worst record the year before at 10-17.

After the game, I had put in an appearance at a postgame gathering for Duke boosters even though Mickie had told me that people would understand if I elected not to show up. "I'm not going to hide from anyone," I told her.

Granted, tucked away in a Denny's at 3:00 A.M. off a secluded stretch of the interstate might seem like I was trying to hide. But I felt it was important to get my staff together quickly before we got back home to Durham.

"Okay, listen up, fellas," I said to them. "We aren't going to do anything desperate. We aren't recruiting anyone else. That's why we recruited these players. If we coach them well, I believe they'll win. If they don't win, I'm not a very good basketball coach. Actually, I know they'll win—because I *know* I'm a damn good coach."

At that point, Johnny Moore, our promotions director, held up his glass of iced tea and said: "Okay, here's to forgetting tonight ever happened."

Then I held up my own glass and said: "Here's to *never* forgetting tonight happened. Not ever."

Courage

There weren't a lot of people believing in me back then. We had experienced two losing seasons in a row and some hard-core fans and supporters were calling for my head.

But my athletic director, Tom Butters, stood by me—as did our assistant coaches and players. And of course, Mickie, our daughters, my mom, and my brother and his family were always there.

A lot of people in the press were saying that there was no way Duke basketball could have a winning season anytime soon—not with that guy with the unpronounceable name running the show. Well, during those tough times, I really believed we were going to have a successful program. I just knew we were not going to fail. And rather than feeling sorry for myself with all of the negative press and doomsday prognosticators, I actually got a little mad. Part of my encouragement to the staff when we were at Denny's was due to anger. Essentially, I wanted to prove wrong everyone who was claiming that there was no way we could ever be successful.

Another part of it was that I just didn't feel we should wallow in, or worry about, things we couldn't do anything about. We couldn't really do much about what people said about us. All we could do was learn from the adversity we experienced, try to handle it with grace, and then get on with our work.

The year after we lost that game to Virginia, we used it as a motivator, not just for our opponents, but for ourselves. I wanted our star players, Johnny Dawkins, Mark Alarie, Jay Bilas, and David Henderson, to remember how that loss felt. And when we eventually started to win, they appreciated it that much more. Not only that, but all of us had to remember how much work it took to win—and to keep on winning.

Courage is a word that comes up a lot in leadership. And it does take courage to walk down that dark alley where others don't want to go. But true bravery in leadership really revolves around the degree to which a person maintains the courage of his convictions.

That kind of courage takes persistence to keep believing in yourself—and resilience to keep picking yourself up after every loss, every stumble, every fall. Following through with your plans, your commitments, your dreams—even when everyone else is saying you can't do it—that's courage.

And why does a leader need courage?

Because somebody is always trying to pull you down when you're a leader. And you cannot be vacillating back and forth with the wind.

There can be a wind where you're successful and everyone agrees with you. Or there can be a wind where you're not successful and everybody disagrees with you. Courage gives a leader the ability to stand straight and not sway no matter which way the wind blows.

A strong gale might change a leader's strategy, but it should never change his core beliefs. If you believe in your system, in the people around you, and in your own abilities, then going 11-17 will not change what you do. But if you don't believe in those things, if you don't have the courage of your convictions, then going 11-17 might change *everything* you do.

At Denny's in 1983 I stuck with my core beliefs, I stuck with the players we recruited, and I told them that I believed they would be successful. And they were. That same team that went 11-17 as freshmen went on to be 37-3 in 1986 when they were seniors. They finished the regular season ranked number one in the national polls, went to the Final Four, and lost in the national championship game to Louisville.

A leader has to know who he is and what he stands for. And he also has to say it, demonstrate it, and mean it if he ever hopes for people to follow him. And, believe me, when you stand strong in those vacillating winds for the first time, it's easier to have courage again and again.

Confidence

In 1998, when Elton Brand completed his freshman year, the press, the sports analysts, everybody said that he was a great, great basketball player. I knew he was *going to be* a great player. But Elton himself did not yet know it.

Because he was out with an injury for seven weeks of the season, when he finally did come back, he wasn't the dominant player that he could have been. He simply wasn't up to

225

par physically. So he just naturally figured that he wasn't as good as everybody was saying he was.

That summer, Elton had a mental obstacle to overcome. He had to overcome the thought that his reputation was better than he really was.

So Elton and I sat down in my office one day and talked about it. He told me that his dream was to play in the NBA, but he didn't know if he'd ever be good enough. I told him that he would definitely be good enough to make it to the NBA and that everything the media was saying about him was true. He just had not come all the way back from his injury. So I advised him to play some off-season basketball.

"You should go to the tryouts for the Goodwill Games," I told him. "You have to make that team and you have to be a key player on it."

Several weeks later, when he made the team, I flew up to New York to watch some of his practices and take in a few of his games. The main reason I did that was so I could reinforce to him that he was good—*really good* at playing basketball.

You can talk about a pitcher throwing shutouts or striking out twelve batters in a game. But until that pitcher does it, he never really knows he's that good. Elton Brand did not know he was that good. We utilized the summer, then, for him to get to know that he was an outstanding player. He had to have the confidence in himself in order to realize his own full potential—in order to achieve his true greatness.

As a leader, I have to have confidence in myself. That goes without saying. But I also want my players to have confidence in themselves. If I'm a manager of a company and I have a terrific director of personnel, I want him to think he's great, too. I want him to think he's so great that he'll set the world on fire.

So how do I make sure he knows it? Well, it's important for me to tell him what I think. But simply telling him that he's terrific won't really accomplish all that much except that he knows how I feel. In order for him to know deep within himself that he's really good, he has to prove it to himself. So my job as a leader is to put him in the position where he can do so.

That's what I did for Elton Brand. I advised him to participate in the Goodwill Games because I was certain he would shine in that venue. And he did shine. In fact, he was a star. So when he came back to Duke for his sophomore year, he was armed with the confidence that comes from experience and knowing.

And Elton had a great, great year in 1999. We made it to the Final Four where we lost a thriller to UConn in the championship game. We finished ranked number one in the final regular season poll with a 37-2 record (which equaled our 1986 team for the most wins in NCAA history). And Elton Brand was named Player of the Year. Neither he nor Duke would have had that great year if he had not played in the Goodwill Games. Elton and I both know that.

With accomplishment comes confidence and with confidence comes belief. It has to be in that order.

Continual Learning

In 1992, Duke basketball won our second national championship in a row. At age forty-five, I was still a fairly young coach to have achieved that kind of success. So where was I supposed to go to learn after that? How does a successful leader continue to get better?

Well, I was fortunate to have been asked to be an assistant coach under Chuck Daly for the 1992 Olympic Dream Team. What an honor that was for me. But even after winning two national championships and being at the top of my profession in college, I went into a situation where I was low man on the totem pole for a couple of months.

The summer of 1992 was an amazing time for my own personal growth. I not only had the privilege of serving with Chuck Daly, Lenny Wilkens, and P. J. Carlesimo on the coaching staff, I was surrounded by some of the greatest basketball talent in history—people like Magic Johnson, Michael Jordan, Larry Bird, David Robinson.

When I worked with all these players, they'd show me great respect. They'd say, "Thanks, Coach," after we had a work session together—and they'd compliment my knowledge of the game.

Together, we created an atmosphere where we kept things simple but organized. And we were able to take a group of extraordinarily talented individuals, pull ourselves together into a fist to play as one—and then go to Barcelona and win the Olympic gold medal for our country. It was one of the proudest moments of my life.

The professionalism that was there through the summer really helped me gain a deeper feeling about my sport. And the relationships I developed during those couple of months were wonderful for me—and have lasted.

But I guess one of the real advantages of that summer was the reinforced confidence I experienced. People had been saying for years that I would be a good coach in the NBA, that I could go there and make a lot of money and win. And over the years, I've turned down several lucrative offers from various NBA teams. The big money has never been a motivating factor for me. But I always wondered how it would be. It was always the challenge that interested me.

Working with the pros on the Dream Team, both coaches and players, helped me understand and believe that I could, in fact, be a good coach in the NBA. In essence, I utilized the summer of 1992 to help develop my own confidence. And it made me stronger when I returned to Duke that next fall.

With the Dream Team, I was in a situation where I could learn something new. And that is something I try to do every spring and summer—after regular and postseason play are completed.

I'll accept a few speaking engagements, for instance. Ever since we won our first national championship, I've received hundreds of requests to speak every year. People feel like I've seen the Holy Grail. "Well, come tell us what it looks like. Tell us how you found it."

I speak to groups that I think I might be able to learn something from. Sometimes bankers or big sales corporations have problems with media, people, or management. So we'll talk about things and I'll get some ideas on how they handled their problems successfully—or hear about some things that didn't work very well. In doing this, I'm not only helping the group I'm speaking to, I'm also able to analyze myself by seeing how I can learn and get better.

Another thing I'll do in the summer is run a few one-man, one-day clinics for other coaches. I basically tell them what we do at Duke and then get into a question-and-answer session.

Sometimes, even though I thought I had explained a theory pretty well, the other coaches will ask for more clarification. And I'll think to myself, "Gee, maybe I need to learn how to explain it better." And sometimes, in preparing for a clinic, I'll remember something that I did in the past. "Why don't I use this drill anymore?" I'll ask myself. "I used to run it all the time and it worked real well."

There has never been a time when I spoke at a clinic that I didn't learn something new. I learn something every single time. That's one of the reasons I do the clinics.

I will also ask people for advice on a regular basis. I have several good friends, for example, who are scouts in the pros. So I'll ask them to come in and watch a practice, or look at some tapes with me, or just sit down and discuss the upcoming season. I try to get their perspective because they're outsiders who don't see our team on a day-to-day basis.

"Okay, you guys have seen a lot of other teams. How do we compare? Are we working as hard as they are?"

Often, there's a tendency for a coach to get stuck in his own little world and think that he's doing just fine. Well, maybe he's not. Maybe he's doing worse than okay. Maybe he's doing better than okay. But how will he ever know unless he checks out what is going on elsewhere in other similar programs? One of the ways to do that is to ask the advice of professionals who are exposed to other similar organizations.

There is a perception out there that once people get out of college, they stop learning. Well I've learned a heck of a lot in my twenty years at Duke and I know I have more to learn.

I feel that I still have more potential to fill. And I often ask myself if anyone can really fulfill his potential. There always seems to be something that can be done better.

When we're born, are we given three baskets of potential? Do we stay with three baskets our entire lives? Or when we fill up two of those baskets, have we developed even more possibilities so that now we have eight baskets of potential? Maybe one of the potentials in the third basket is to learn how to make more baskets.

I feel like I have a lot more potential at this stage of my life. Of course, I may be less likely to set the world record in a 100 meter dash. Some of the baskets that contained physical potential are full. But scientists say that we use only 10 percent of our brain, so there have to be other things that can be focused on and then achieved.

The beauty of leadership is that there are no complete or perfect recipes. You cannot say: "Do these ten things and you will be a leader." Those ten things might help you become a leader, but doing them alone won't make you one.

Any blueprint to leadership has to be used as a guide. It can only be structured so much. There has to be room for personal creativity. And every leader has to put his own signature on his leadership style.

Continual learning is a key to effective leadership because no one can know everything there is to know. In leadership, things change. Events change, circumstances change, people change. As a matter of fact, leadership is all about change. Leaders take people to places they've never been before.

Because leaders are always encountering new situations, they have to learn how to meet new challenges, to adapt, to confront, to master, to win. A leader's job is ongoing. It's like a ring. There is no end. Leadership never stops.

We have to think of different ways to learn and grow every day. Because when you stop growing, you start to decay. And life goes on, win or lose. Either way, you just have to try to figure out what you can do better the next time.

I believe every person has to learn from success and failure. That's why when my staff and I were at Denny's, I did not want any of us to forget that terrible loss to Virginia.

We should never forget a defeat. Defeat can be the key to future victory.

231

Hard Work

My mom and dad never missed a day of work cleaning floors and operating the elevator. If they were coughing or sniffling in the morning, it was: "I gotta go to work." If one of them had a fever, it was: "I gotta go to work." They never missed work—I mean, *never.*

And I never missed school when I was a kid. If I'd wake up in the morning with a fever and said I needed to stay home because I was sick, they'd say: "What, I paid for you to go to school and you're not going to go to school? Here, drink a cup of Polish tea and sweat it out. You're going to school."

That's what I learned growing up. Show up every day, even if you have to sweat it out. And you know what? I became amazingly dependable—just like my parents.

For some reason, "hard" and "work" have been associated with other four-letter words that have negative connotations. But I believe work is good. There is dignity in work. I also believe that a hard-work ethic forges strong leaders.

I have found that when people achieve something that they've really worked hard for, it makes them feel great, superb, wonderful. In that context, rather than causing pain, work brings people joy, fulfillment, and self-esteem.

"You mean if we get that done, we're going to feel great? And it'll take only four hours? Well, then, let's get it done!"

It's like the craftsman who did the woodwork on the altar at the Duke Chapel. He spent countless hours, days, weeks, months working on it. When he got it done, he surely felt great about it. He was proud of it. His signature was on it.

In order to be a winner, you have to look for ways of getting things done and not for reasons why things can't be done.

People who live with excuses have things that can't be done hovering around them all the time.

The only way we lose is if we don't try our best. There is always a way to win. Never say you cannot do it. Find the way to win.

Honesty and Integrity

A lot of our success in Duke basketball has to do with character. And at the heart of character is honesty and integrity.

We all know what honesty means. And integrity is nothing more than doing the right thing no matter who's watching you. Are you going to show integrity only when someone is watching you—or are you going to show it all the time?

In our program, the truth is the basis of all that we do. There is nothing more important than the truth because there's nothing more powerful than the truth. Consequently, on our team, we always tell one another the truth. We *must* be honest with one another. There is no other way.

In addition, as a leader, I believe I must be honest with myself. If a leader is honest with himself, it'll be a lot easier to be honest with everybody else. I consider my biggest achievement to be any time a kid knows I've been honest with him.

Whenever I go back to Chicago, I find myself thinking, "Gee, I'm so lucky, it's amazing."

Not because my family was poor or that I had humble beginnings—but, rather, that I had it so good. And also because of all those values my folks taught me. They were great values—and they proved to be the basis for how I would conduct myself for the rest of my life.

233

Back then, you grew up believing in God, you told the truth—and you loved your country and playground basketball.

It was really very simple.

COACH K's TIPS

- True bravery in leadership revolves around the degree to which a person maintains the courage of his convictions.

- When you stand strong in those vacillating winds for the first time, it's easier to have courage again and again.

- People must have confidence in themselves before they can realize their full potential.

- Put yourself in a situation where you can learn something new.

- Never forget a defeat. Defeat can be the key to victory.

- When you stop growing, you start to decay.

- When people achieve something that they've really worked hard for, it makes them feel great, superb, wonderful.

- The only way you lose is if you don't try your best.

- Integrity is nothing more than doing the right thing no matter who's watching you.

- Make the truth the basis of all you do.

15

FRIENDSHIP

"Life changes when you least expect it to. The future is uncertain. So, seize this day, seize this moment, and make the most of it."

—Jim Valvano

"Please, God, can you do something for Jim? And thank you for allowing me to have this time with him."

—Coach K

"Friendships, along with love, make life worth living."

—Coach K

*I*n March 1999, Duke defeated Temple in the NCAA East Regional championship game—which sent us to the Final Four. During the last minute of the contest, it was clear we were going to win, so we started substituting for the starters.

As I turned to my right on the bench, I noticed that our lead assistant coach, Quin Snyder, had tears streaming down his cheeks. So I put my arm around him and said: "Now you know what it feels like to coach."

Quin wasn't crying because he was going to the Final Four. He was crying for the kids on our team who had worked so hard all year long and were now realizing their collective dream.

That moment was innocence. It was purity. And it was filled with love. You cannot buy a feeling like that.

"We Will Always Be Friends"

After the 1999 Final Four, Quin Snyder was offered the position of head basketball coach at the University of Missouri. I was so proud of him, so happy for him.

When he came over and told me about the offer, my mind drifted back ten years to the senior speech he made at our annual awards banquet in 1989. He had just completed four years as a player and he was struggling to explain what it had meant to him.

"Coach, in this case, language is insufficient," he said gazing in my direction. "Words fall way short when I try to describe the emotion I feel for you. Last night, I began to remember some of the words you use to help us win games. But winning games was really secondary. They were words that you used to instill values in us that we will carry with us forever. I'd like to repeat some of those words.

"Commitment, integrity, toughness, honesty, collective responsibility, pride, and love. After each word, you feel a different emotion. And to me, those words and those emotions are Duke basketball. But there's one word that I saved for last—because that word meant more to me than all the rest.

"In a hotel room in Seattle, you used the word 'friend.' It's that word I'll remember above and beyond the others. It's that word I'll always remember and cherish."

The conversation in Seattle to which Quin referred had taken place only the previous week. We had just lost in the semifinals of the Final Four to Seton Hall, which, of course, ended our season. Quin had taken the loss particularly hard because he was from Mercer Island, Washington, and had been playing in front of his friends and family. After we got back to the hotel, I pulled all the guys together for a chat. 239

"Look, I don't want any of you to walk out of this room blaming yourselves," I told them. "Don't worry about whether you missed a shot or didn't get a key rebound. Rather, I want you to take away the memory that you all had a great year. And we really did have a great year. So we're going to stay here in Seattle. I want you to take time to be with your families over the next few days. And I want you to be here for the national championship game on Monday night. Because, someday, we're going to win the national championship. And I want you to know what it will be like to experience being there.

"One more thing before you leave, guys. I want you to remember that you have a friend. I'm your friend. No matter what happens, we'll always be friends."

Friendship has always been important to me. From the Columbo days in Chicago with Moe Mlynski and my other buddies—through high school, West Point, and my tenure at Duke as a head basketball coach. All of the players, the coaches, the secretaries, the managers—they're all my friends. And I work hard at staying in regular contact with them so that the relationships will continue and live on.

When Friends Leave

At the conclusion of the 1999 season, Quin wasn't the only person in our organization to move on. We also lost seven players. Three of the guys, Trajan Langdon, Taymon Domzalski, and Justin Caldbeck, were departing seniors. But four others, Elton Brand, William Avery, Corey Maggette, and Chris Burgess, were rising juniors and sophomores. For their own reasons, they decided either to go pro or transfer out.

In Elton Brand's case, I already knew that he and his

mother wanted him to go to the NBA. But they struggled with their decision. They were sensitive to the fact that no Duke basketball player had ever before left early to go pro and they didn't want to hurt anybody.

Well, I didn't want Elton and his mom to feel guilty. I knew this was going to happen and I wanted to make it a joyous occasion for them. So, a few days after I had hip replacement surgery, I asked them to come to the hospital.

"Look, you want to do this, don't you, Elton?" I asked.

"Yes, Coach," he replied.

"But we don't want it to hurt Duke," said his mom.

"If it's what is best for the two of you," I said, "Duke will be fine with it and so will I."

I wanted a relationship of the highest order with Elton Brand and his mother for the rest of our lives. How I handled that situation would determine that future. We were not going to get a different ending. And you know what? I didn't want a different ending because it was supposed to happen at that moment. Besides, when the next superstar kid comes out of Peekskill High School and goes to Elton Brand to ask about Coach K and Duke University, I trust that Elton will say we treated him great and did the right thing.

So I was faced with the loss of Brand, Avery, Maggette, Burgess, three departing seniors—and I had to recuperate from hip replacement surgery. One of the first actions I took after leaving the hospital was to rally our three new team captains together. Shane Battier, Chris Carrawell, and Nate James came over to my house and we discussed what had happened and why it happened. But that part of the conversation lasted maybe ten minutes or so. The rest of the ninety-minute meeting concentrated on how we were going to prepare for next season.

I told them that we were going to be good regardless of the loss we'd suffered. In fact, with the outstanding new recruits we had coming in, I told them that the potential was there to have a really great year. But it would take a lot of work from the three of them. Then I asked them, "Do you believe we can do that?" And I'll never forget what Chris Carrawell said to me in response. "Coach," he said, "I believe it because you said it!"

I was proud that the new team captains were able to put this situation behind them just like they would put any loss of a game during the regular season behind them. After all, they were losing seven members of their team—all of whom were their friends. I was also gratified that my relationship with these three guys had grown to the point where we trusted one another like friends *should* trust one another.

When I look back on the loss of those four additional players from our 1999 team, I really believe the biggest loss was the friendship that would have developed if they had stayed for the full four years. That was the worst part of it for me.

I was, of course, concerned about the loss of potential the team had for the next year. But I wasn't devastated. In truth, as soon as their decisions were made, I immediately began working on recruiting. Many people said to me: "Wow, that's too bad. Look at what you could have had next year." But I was looking at what I *did* have—and what I was going to do with it.

Because things change by the hour in my business, I've learned to live with instability and deal with it. In this case, I wished the departing players all the best and tried to keep in touch with the ones who wanted to maintain our friendships. People must do what they feel is right for them—even if it sometimes means breaking a commitment they've previously made.

After Corey Maggette decided to go pro, he and his family came over to my house for a visit. "I want you to know this," I said to him. "You are going to be entering a world where the truth is not always embraced. If you ever want help or advice, I'll be there for you. And I'll tell you the truth."

And that's the way I feel toward all of them.

Leaders are often faced with situations like this one. For me, however, it was the first time it happened in my entire twenty-four-year coaching career. I had never had even one player leave early for the pros. It would be equivalent to a business losing several of its top performers to another company because they received a better financial offer or a bigger compensation package.

Sometimes, all the good things we try to provide for our team members, all the things we try to teach them—the values, the words Quin Snyder mentioned in his speech—do not make a difference. Sometimes, people simply have to do what they have to do. Sometimes, they have to move on.

So how do leaders handle it?

Well, we feel sad, disappointed, possibly betrayed. But real leaders have to put all those feelings behind them. They have to thank the players for doing a great job while they were with us—and wish them well. Then we have to get on with it.

It's always "next season, next game, next play."

And we should never hold a grudge. We should try to preserve our friendships, because friendships, along with love, make life worth living. If I couldn't have the friendships and the love, I think I would tire of coaching.

243

Jim Valvano

I've experienced many different relationships in my fifty-plus years. And I've enjoyed them all. But the best form of friendship I ever encountered was during the last six months of Jim Valvano's life.

Jim and I played basketball games against each other when we were in college. He was at Rutgers, I was at Army—and we were both point guards and team leaders. We also coached against each other in our early years when he led Iona's basketball team and I was the head coach at West Point.

There were a lot of similarities between us. We both hailed from close families in large ethnic neighborhoods. He was from a big Italian family in New York, I was from a big Polish family in Chicago. We both married and had three daughters. We both were very passionate about what we did—although Jim was more outgoing and flamboyant. I was more reserved, more coat-and-tie.

Our styles of coaching were similar to our personalities, which, of course, meant that our teams played differently. And that became obvious beginning with the 1980–1981 season when he and I both came to the Atlantic Coast Conference—Jim as the head coach at North Carolina State University and I at Duke.

Back then, the ACC was the top basketball conference in the country with some of the top coaches: Terry Holland at Virginia, Lefty Dreisell at Maryland, Bill Foster at Clemson, and, of course, the renowned Dean Smith of North Carolina. Along with Bobby Cremins, who came to Georgia Tech a year later, Jim and I were like a new breed coming into the ACC. We didn't worry so much about the fact that North Carolina's program and Dean Smith himself were legendary. We understood it and respected it, but there was no fear of it.

We were two young guys in our early thirties, the two new kids on the block—so I think Jim and I gravitated toward each other—just like we would have if we'd met on the playground when we were eight or nine years old. But while I usually wanted to be the diplomat, Jimmy always wanted to stir up a little trouble.

During a recess in some stodgy ACC meetings, for instance, we'd get together and commiserate with each other. "Can you believe all that crap?" we'd say. "What the hell's going on here?" "Tell you what, when we get back, you bring up this particular subject and I'll bring up that other subject—and we'll cover each other's back. Okay?" "Right."

We used to do a lot of that kind of stuff—and it was fun.

At other times, though, we acted like the Little Rascals. In fact, sometimes, we were downright irreverent. I remember how Jimmy used to roll his eyes at the beginning of every ACC coaches meeting because Dean Smith was always the last one to come into the room. It was like the world champ coming into the ring last. Well, one time, Valvano grabbed Cremins and me before the start of a meeting.

"Hey, listen, we're not going to let Dean be the last one into the meeting this time. Come with me."

So the three of us hid out in the men's room down the corridor. We waited and we waited for what seemed like an inordinately long period of time. Finally, Dean showed up and went into the room. Then Jimmy, Bobby, and I sneaked out of the bathroom and waltzed into the meeting. Valvano came in last and, with a big grin on his face, closed the door.

Jim and I always got along real well. We had a lot of respect for each other although, early on, it was a grudging kind of

245

respect. After all, we were building our own programs and competing against each other. And, over the years, we both achieved a lot of success. But it was Jimmy who had success earlier.

While I was struggling with two miserable losing seasons, he seemed to rocket right to the top. In 1983, the same year Duke was 11-17 and I was huddled at Denny's with my staff, Valvano and North Carolina State won the national championship.

I can remember flying on a plane with him back in 1991 after Duke had won our first national title. We had both been bumped up to first class and we just sat there and talked for several hours.

"I want to thank you for winning the national championship in 1983," I said to him at one point in the conversation. "You saved my job!"

"What are you talking about?" he asked with a bewildered look on his face.

"Well, because there was so much media attention about NC State's run for the national championship—winning so many close games, winning the ACC tournament, the whole Cinderella story—there wasn't enough space to write anything about how bad Duke was.

"So you see, Jim," I said with a grin, "you saved my job."

"Mike," he replied, "we're in our early forties now and you know what's wrong with us? We did too much too soon."

"What do you mean?"

"We were too successful too soon. And now everybody expects that all the time from us. We should have waited until we were in our mid-fifties. The other coaches, who may only go 20-12, are not expected to win it all every year. Now, we are."

"Yeah, I guess you're right. We put the bar very high at an early age, didn't we?"

And then Jim looked me square in the eye and said, "I don't know if I'm going to keep doing this. Coaching, I mean."

That was a major statement for him to make because Jimmy loved coaching so much. But he also loved other things. He had so many ideas floating around in his head, I believe he just felt he had to get out and give some of them a try.

Shortly thereafter, while still head basketball coach at NC State, he took on the duties of athletic director. But some people didn't think that was such a good idea. And because Jim Valvano was not a whisperer—but a talker, almost an entertainer in some regards—a number of petty people set out to tear him down. He was scrutinized unmercifully, for instance, in a horrible book that alleged cheating and cutting corners in recruiting.

The subsequent chain of events began to take a toll on Jim's life, his family, and his reputation. He was terribly stressed about the whole thing and circumstances forced him to leave NC State. He became a broadcaster for ABC and ESPN and he was great at it. He knew the game, he came across well, he was passionate. All in all, Jim Valvano was terrific on television.

He and I became even closer after that. I think the fact that we were no longer competing with each other had something to do with it. There were no longer any invisible barriers between us.

I'm really glad Jim followed his heart and became a television broadcaster. I'm also really glad, even though he lamented it, that he had so much early success in his coaching career. Because, unfortunately, Jim did not live into his mid-fifties.

In the summer of 1992, he began experiencing some pain in his lower back. A battery of tests revealed that he had a rare form of cancer that was based in the bones.

When we first heard about it, Mickie and I didn't think of it as horrible. We thought, "Well, he's young, they caught it early, they'll take care of it." But our daughter Jamie, who was eleven at the time, was worried. As a matter of fact, she wrote an essay for a school project entitled "Stress Causes Cancer," in which she speculated that the media caused so much stress in Jim's life that he contracted cancer.

Jimmy didn't make a big to-do about it. But it wasn't long before we found out that he was having a really tough time. He was experiencing a great deal of pain, but he kept doing his job on television and would never let the viewers see how ill he really was.

He was employing that old coaching maxim, "show strength, hide weakness."

One day, I invited Jim to one of our basketball practices. Afterward, I asked him if he would like to speak to the team— and he said, "Sure." But I had no idea how emotional and moving his words would be. They remain etched in my memory to this day.

"Fellas," he began, "life changes when you least expect it to. Right now, my goal in life is to be able to come back and talk to you guys again next season.

"You don't know. You *never* know what's going to happen tomorrow. I've always been a person who's tried to pack everything into the moment. I want to do it more and more now because the future is uncertain for me.

"Why don't you do that?" he asked the kids. "The future should always be uncertain for you. You never know what's going to happen next. Don't ever think that this day doesn't mean anything. It means a lot. Don't think you have an infinite amount of days left. You don't. So, seize this day, seize this moment, and make the most of it."

Jim didn't say much. He didn't have to. But I looked at guys on our team and could see their eyes welling up with tears. Jim had touched their hearts with his sincerity and his eloquence.

And then Jimmy took off his jacket, loosened his tie, and began interacting with the kids. For the next hour or so, he joked with them, worked with them on some drills and techniques, shot a few hoops. He was on the playground again. He was coaching again. He was having fun.

As we walked off the court together, he was holding his jacket over his shoulder and he had a smile on his face.

I put my arm around him and said, "Thanks, Jim. That was really good for our guys."

"That was really good for me, Mike," he replied. "I loved that."

It was a short time thereafter that he began receiving treatment at Duke University Medical Center. When I first started visiting him at the hospital, I wasn't sure if he really wanted me there—or if I should drop by too often. But it quickly became obvious that he did want me there. So during the season, I went over as many times a week as I could manage. And after the season concluded, I was over there just about every day.

During those visits, Jim and I really connected. We sat and talked for hours about coaching and basketball, about our families and life. You name it, we talked about it. In fact, once we started talking, he wanted everyone else to leave—even Pam, his wife. So Pam and his family would sometimes sit in the waiting room across the hall—and they'd hear a lot of noise coming from Jim's room as he got louder and more animated.

Those visits really picked up his spirits. He'd tell stories, do impersonations of other coaches and referees, relive great moments in his life and career. In essence, Jimmy was going through his whole life with me. And when I walked out of his room, I would either be laughing or crying.

At one point, I recall asking him, "How the hell do you feel, Jim? I mean really."

"Jesus, Mike, my back is killing me. I'm scared to death."

And then he said that this feeling reminded him of some time in the past—and, all of a sudden, he'd bolt off into a story. He'd forget about the pain while he was telling his story and, the next thing you know, we'd be laughing.

He was a coach. So he tried to turn something negative and bad into something positive and good.

Another time, he blurted out, "Mike, I'm afraid. I'm afraid of dying. I don't want to die, but I know I'm going to die."

And then, just as quickly, he started talking about how some people handled this whole "cancer thing," as he put it.

"I wish everybody would take it on like coaches," he told me. "They should come in and say, 'Let's try something different.' 'Let's try something new.' I'm not afraid to try anything. Just like in coaching, if something isn't working, we innovate. We try *anything* that will help. In coaching, we never give up. Never!

"And Mike," he continued with a look of astonishment, "sometimes, people come in here with frowns or sad looks on their faces. Can you believe it? Why would I want to see people down? I would never do that for my team. I would never want them to see me and think, 'Oh, man, we're going to lose today.'"

Jim Valvano was a coach. And a coach has to show the face his team needs to see.

When I walked out of his room after that particular conversation, I talked to the doctors and nurses. "I know you have a bunch of bad days around here, but try not to be down around him," I told them. "When you go into Jim's room, be up. That's what he wants. Try to cheer him up a little bit, okay?"

I knew Jim was trying his level best to beat cancer. He couldn't believe that "this damned disease," as he put it, was going to get the best of him. That was simply unacceptable. So he just kept saying that there had to be a way to beat cancer. There had to be.

Jim Valvano was a coach. He was trying to find a way to win. So he came up with a game plan.

One day I walked into his room and he went through the elements of his strategy.

"You know what," he said, "I want to start a foundation. I'd like for you to be on it, Mike. My vision of this is that it would be a foundation for cancer research. But I don't want it to be run the way they normally run these things. I'd like to have a foundation where we could give money to doctors and researchers who are trying to find cures in new and creative ways. The government only awards money to one out of six people who apply for grants on cancer research. What about those other five people? That's totally unacceptable for me. Grants are usually about $50,000. That doesn't seem like so much. We can raise that.

"Cancer hits everybody. There's got to be a way, through this foundation, that we can give money directly to a researcher with an innovative idea—one that might just end up 251 being the cure. I can't find the cure myself, but I can sure as hell get money for people who might be able to do it."

I recall walking out of his room that day, going to my car, and just sitting there behind the wheel thinking about what he had just told me. And I crossed myself and said a prayer.

"Please, God, can you do something for Jim? And thank you for allowing me to have this time with him."

Here was this amazing human being, my friend Jimmy Valvano, lying in his bed dying of incurable cancer. He knew that no matter what he did, he was going to die. He had every excuse in the world to have a bad attitude. He had every excuse to blame somebody, to feel sorry for himself.

But Jim was a coach. "No excuses, sir. No excuses."

So he devised a game plan that could win even if he wasn't around. In other words, he was saying, "Even though I'm not here physically, I'm going to beat this damn thing after I die— so that it will help other people who may find themselves in the same situation."

Part of being a coach is to have empathy for other people. And, boy, did Jim Valvano ever care about other people. In this case, he was caring for people he had never before met. He was caring for people who weren't even born yet.

For him to have that idea was amazing. Simply amazing. He used the last couple months of his life to create a stepping-stone to cure cancer. His game plan was the formation of the Jimmy V Foundation. It was a game plan that would keep going long after he was gone. A game plan that I think will eventually win.

Jim Valvano's last game was his best game.

On the morning of April 28, 1993, I was in my office when I got a call from the hospital.

"It's near the end. Come quickly."

I sprinted across the campus to the hospital and walked into his room. Jim was lying unconscious and quiet. Pam and their three daughters were with him. I came in and gave some hugs to try to console them. But mostly, I tried to stay in the background.

Jim was alternately quiet and incoherent. Then he started shaking a little bit—and, suddenly, it was all over.

And I was stunned. I couldn't believe it. I just couldn't believe it.

Even though everybody was expecting it, a part of me would not accept the fact that Jim was going to die. I guess it has to do with being a coach. We never think about losing. We always feel we're going to win—especially if a person has the will to win. And Jim certainly had that will. But he was suffering. He really took a beating during those final few months.

I just kept thinking that he's too young. He's got too much to give. This can't happen. It wasn't the time. It seemed that he should have so much more time, that his family should have so much more time together with him.

But all of a sudden, time had run out. The game was over. At that moment, it ended completely for him.

And I never felt so helpless in my entire life.

A coach is supposed to know what to do. But I had no clue what to do. I felt like I was no help to anybody. I believe my being there was comforting to Pam, but I felt like I should have faded into the wall. I felt so powerless to do anything that might have been of consequence during those next few moments.

I didn't want to accept that my friend was dead—even though he was lying right there in front of me. And as I looked on the scene with his family, I felt so bad for them. I felt so bad.

When I finally left the hospital, I meandered back across

253

campus by myself. Actually, it wasn't so much of a walk as it was a time alone. I didn't want to be with anyone. I just wanted to be with the thought of Jim.

It was a beautiful spring day. The sun was shining, the trees were budding, flowers were blooming. Birds were chirping and squirrels were running around. It was a day fitting for the memory of Jim Valvano—full of life, full of joy, full of beauty.

On that stroll, I started thinking about things that there are no answers for. Why did it happen to Jim and not me? Same age, same type of background, same profession, so many similarities. Why him and not me?

I guess that's where faith has to come in. I had no answers, so I said a prayer for my friend—and for me.

"Please, God, have him with you. Protect him now that his pain is over. And give me better insight into what I'm doing— so that I'll understand that there will be a final day with my family. And that, before that final day, can we have as much life and as much togetherness as we possibly can?"

I was pretty quiet for a long period of time after Jim's death.

I reflected on the last six months of his life, the time we spent together, all of our conversations. And there are two things he said to me that come to the forefront.

"I didn't do it right," he said, referring to the fact that he spent too much time trying to achieve and too little time taking care of himself and his family. "I was really wrong. Don't screw it up, Mike."

Another statement he made was, "A person really doesn't become whole until he becomes a part of something that's bigger than himself."

Sometimes, when I think of those remarks, I just want to

take my family and go back to the old neighborhood in Chicago and coach.

Sometimes, I just want to be back on the school playground with Moe and the rest of the Columbos.

Once in a while, when I'm in church, I'll light a candle for my friend Jimmy. I'll think about him, about our time together, and about our very special friendship.

It's friendships. Friendships are the best.

COACH K's TIPS

- You have to work hard at staying in contact with your friends so that the relationships will continue and live on.

- Sometimes, all the good things you try to provide for your team members do not make a difference. Sometimes, people have to move on.

- Leaders have to learn to live with instability.

- When people leave, thank them for doing a great job and wish them well. Hold no grudges.

- Friendships, along with love, make life worth living.

- Pack everything into the moment. The future should always be uncertain for you.

- Touch people's hearts with sincerity and eloquence.

- If something isn't working, try something new and different. Innovate. Never give up. Never.

- Part of being a leader is to have empathy for people.

- Make your last game your best game.

- Find a way to win.

16

LIFE

"Michael, I've never said this to you in our whole married life before, but it's me or basketball right now. If you don't show up at the doctor's office at 2:30, I'll know what your choice was."

—**Mickie Krzyzewski**

"Since I came back from my season out, I constantly ask myself, 'What's your job, knucklehead?' And I try to keep a balance with all the people and things I love in my life."

—**Coach K**

"Coaching basketball is my vehicle for life—for the larger journey."

—**Coach K**

*I*n January 1995, after barely one third of the regular season, we had just been beaten by Clemson, 75–70, at Cameron Indoor Stadium in a loss that lowered our record to 9-3. After the game, our assistant coaches gathered at my house, as usual, to review and analyze the loss and figure out how we could get better.

"I want all you guys to sit down," I said to Mike Brey, Pete Gaudet, and Tommy Amaker. Mickie was also in the room. Then I moved to a place where I could look directly into all their faces.

"I'm going to resign tomorrow," I said after drawing a deep breath.

"I've always believed that the group is more important than any single person. Duke deserves the best. Well, I can no longer do my best. I can't even be mediocre right now."

Everyone sat there in stunned silence. Tommy Amaker looked at Mickie to gauge her reaction. "I remember she just dropped her head in her hands and said, 'Oh, Michael,'" he recalled. "Then I knew this was no reaction to a single loss. It was clearly something that went much deeper."

And I was very serious. After the Clemson game, I had absolutely no emotion. I felt nothing—and I knew that was not right.

Over the previous several weeks, I had lost a lot of weight and had no energy or passion. I was a physical wreck and I knew for me to continue would be a disservice to my team. It wasn't about quitting, it was the realization that somebody else could do the job better. I had to look after Duke, my program, my guys. It's what I learned in the military. If your people are engaged in competition and you cannot lead them, then you step back and let someone else lead. That was my thought.

Amaker, Gaudet, and Brey all expressed support, but also encouraged me not to act rashly. "Take some time to think it over, Mike," they advised.

"I'm not sure if I want to coach anymore," I said.

"Well, Coach," said Tommy, "you know how you feel better than anybody. But as someone who played for you and has worked for you—and with all due respect—I find it hard to believe that you don't want to coach anymore."

And then Mickie came up to me and gave me a hug. "I'm not going to let you do this," she said. "After all that you've accomplished, all that you've done—you're not going to go out like this."

Adversity

This all had been building for quite some time—ever since the previous summer when I started to experience pains in my left leg. I told my doctor that it was probably a pulled hamstring. So, for three months, that's what I was treated for.

But by September, the pain had not gone away and Mickie reminded me that pulled hamstrings do not last this long. "You need to go to the doctor and get it checked out," she said.

My doctors informed me that I had a disk problem in my back and that the exercises I had been doing for that pulled hamstring were only making it worse, so they recommended some new exercise therapy. But a few weeks later, on a recruiting trip to Kansas City, the disk ruptured and I could barely walk by the time I got off the airplane. My doctors called in a prescription to kill the pain and, when I returned to Durham, they started giving me a series of shots to reduce the swelling.

But things didn't get any better. As a matter of fact, the numbness in my leg seemed to get worse. So I went to a neurosurgeon to have it checked out again. When he told me to stand on my toes with all my weight on my right leg, I did okay. But when he told me to do the same thing with my left leg, I collapsed to the floor. I was stunned.

"What does this mean?" I asked him.

"Well, you've lost your left calf muscle. If you don't want to walk around like Quasimodo for the rest of your life, you'll get surgery."

That scared me. And two days later, on October 23, 1994— eight days after basketball practices began—I had surgery to repair what turned out to be a severely herniated disk. After a few days, I began to feel better. I still wasn't feeling great, but any improvement was a sign to me that I should get back to my team.

The doctors advised me to go slow, to take up to ten weeks of recovery time, and to severely limit my physical activity except, of course, for basic rehabilitation. But I said, "Hey, I'm feeling pretty good. I think I can come back in a week."

"Well," they responded, "then you have to do it on a limited basis. Maybe if you have a special chair there, it'll be okay."

So I got my way—and I was back on the court within ten days.

Unfortunately, over the next two months, I really began to go downhill. I started losing weight. I was getting weaker. The pain in my back was getting worse. And I was exhausted all the time.

By this time, Mickie was furious at both me and the doctors. She didn't like the fact that I was ignoring all their medical advice—and she said the doctors were intimidated by "Coach K" and would not put their foot down to say no. "Any other patient who goes through that type of operation wouldn't be allowed to do what you're doing," she told me. And she was right.

But I kept right on forging ahead.

Our team went on a trip to Hawaii to participate in the Rainbow Classic and we were fortunate enough to win two out of three games. But on the plane for that long eight-hour trip back, I had a terrible time. I couldn't get into any kind of comfortable position. My back was absolutely killing me. And I got no sleep during the entire tournament.

After the plane flight home, I felt completely worn down—both mentally and physically. I had all but stopped eating. I

261

even had a conversation with a friend about my beautiful nine-year-old daughter, Jamie. "I thought Jamie was fourteen," he said. He was right. I wasn't thinking clearly enough to know how old my youngest daughter was.

Then we played the Clemson game, got beat, 75–70, and I told the guys I was going to resign.

Two days later, when I woke up in the morning, I could barely move.

I struggled to get up and shower, but then staggered back into bed. A little while later, I got up and shaved—and staggered back to bed. Then I tried to get up again, pulled on my coaching sweatsuit, and fell back into bed.

Mickie saw me as a broken-down guy—with sunken eyes and a stooped back. And she had had enough.

"I'm setting up an appointment with the doctor and you need to be there," she said.

"I can't. I have to go to practice. I have appointments with the players. And then we're leaving for the Georgia Tech game. I don't have time."

"You don't have the strength," she said before leaving the room to call the doctor.

When she came back, Mickie informed me that the appointment was all set up for 2:30 that afternoon.

"But I told you that I have practice at 2:30!"

"Michael," she said, "I've never said this to you in our whole married life before, but it's me or basketball right now. If you don't show up at 2:30, I'll know what your choice was."

My first reaction to Mickie's ultimatum was anger. "Don't lay that on me," I thought. "Why is she doing this to me today? I don't need this on top of everything else."

But then, when I was driving to my office, I realized for her to make a statement like that, she must have seen something that I did not see—or didn't want to see. I not only trust Mickie, I love her. "I guess I better go to that appointment," I finally decided.

So I asked the assistant coaches to run practice and I went to the 2:30 doctor's appointment. In my fifteen years at Duke, it was the first practice I had ever missed. In fact, I had never before missed a practice in my entire coaching career.

That doctor's appointment was a turning point in my life.

A Season Out

When I walked into Dr. John Feagin's office, he took one look at me and said: "You're going to the hospital. We're going to do a lot of tests and we're going to see just where you're at right now."

He did not even examine me—I looked that bad.

"Okay," I said, "but will you at least let me go back to my office so I can tell the staff that I won't be able to go to Georgia Tech with them?"

Dr. Feagin agreed. "But make it quick," he said.

When I told the staff that I had to check into the hospital and miss the game, I broke down. "I feel like I'm deserting you guys," I said. "I'm sorry, I'm sorry."

It was one of the hardest things I've ever done. All my previous training taught me not to wave to the troops going away—but to be with them. Now I had to let go—and it killed me to have to do it.

But the staff couldn't have been more supportive. "It's okay, Mike. It's okay. Go to the hospital. Let the doctors help you. We'll be okay. Don't worry about a thing. We love you."

So I was hospitalized and, as I underwent nearly every

medical test known to man (including everything from CAT scans to psychological analyses), I got worried. After all, Jimmy Valvano's cancer started with back pain. Was it possible I had cancer? I didn't have an answer. All I knew is that I had never felt so poorly in my life. Never.

Finally, though, the doctors told me that all the tests indicated that my problem stemmed from trying to get back too fast after back surgery. I was trying to do too much too soon, they told me. I was driving myself into the ground.

To me, that meant that all I had to do was rest up a little bit. And I was so relieved to hear that it was not cancer—or another slipped disk, or something equally as bad—that I immediately began to feel a little better.

"Okay, how long do I have to stay here?" I asked. "We've got a game on Tuesday. I should be able to make it, right?"

But this time, the doctors were ready for me.

They decided to form a team so they would be stronger in telling me no. There were five of them. Five—the same number of players on a basketball team. Five—the same number of fingers on a hand. The team consisted of: Dr. John Feagin, the lead physician; Dr. Jean Spaulding, a psychiatrist; Dr. Ralph Snyderman, chancellor for medical affairs at Duke; Dr. Keith Brodie, former president of Duke University, and a close personal friend; and Dr. Jim Clapp, professor of medicine and director of the Duke Center for Living.

This group ganged up on me is what they did. They formed a fist. "Two is better than one if two can act as one." In this case, it was five acting as one. They met several times as a group, conferred, and then called a meeting with me where they lowered the boom.

"First of all, *we're* in charge, not *you*," they said firmly. "You cannot coach for two weeks. Do you understand? You have to take the time to do postoperative rehab *properly*. At the end of that time, we'll reevaluate the situation."

For those next two weeks, I alternately rested and performed physical therapy twice a day. I was not allowed to go to any basketball games or practices. Heck, I wasn't even allowed to speak to any of the players or my staff.

Those two weeks were the most horrible time for me because the team began to fall apart. All I could do was to sit at home and watch them lose ball game after ball game. I remember one game they played against Virginia at Cameron when they were ahead by as many as 25 points. Good, I thought, they're going to start winning again. I don't have to worry. But we ended up losing that game in double overtime—and I was devastated.

My guys were out there having a tough time and I was at home. There was a lot of anxiety on my part. "I need to get back," I kept saying to myself. "I need to get back."

When the two weeks were up, my physical therapist reported that I just was not getting any better. If anything, I was worse. Finally, the doctors called a meeting. "You're not trying to get better, Krzyzewski," they said. "You're trying to get back and you're just making things worse. We need to reverse this process right now. You're out for the whole year. We don't want you to so much as think about coming back until next year. Do you understand? Is that clear?"

I was shocked. I could not fathom sitting out for the entire year. It had never even entered my mind.

But the team made the decision that this is what needed to happen. And they came in, looked me in the eye, and told me so. I had no choice. Mickie was on their side and so were all my friends and associates.

The truth is that I felt relieved. I guess I needed somebody to tell me what to do because I was blinded by my emotions and my commitment not to miss work. I guess it reminded me that even a head coach, like any other leader, has to remember that there are always other people around who can lead—and that we should listen to them.

So I went to my athletic director, Tom Butters, and told him the situation. "Tom, the doctors want me out for the rest of the season. They say I can't get better and coach at the same time. If you want me to resign, I'll understand completely. I'd feel guilty if I didn't tell you that."

After listening intently, Tom put his hand on my shoulder. "Mike, this is your job whenever you're ready to come back. It doesn't matter if it's tomorrow, six weeks from now, six months from now, or six years from now. This is *your* job. I don't want anyone else as Duke's basketball coach."

It was at that point that I started to get better. I finally realized that, for once in my life, I had to be committed to me—and me only. I had to do it in order to get my health back.

I had not taken care of myself. Now it was time to do so.

Lessons Learned

Sitting out the rest of the 1994–1995 season gave me a lot of time to think. And, as I began to rehabilitate properly, I also began to reflect and reevaluate.

I believe people look at things closer when they lose than when they win. At least, that's what I found myself doing. Sometimes when you win, there's stuff under the couch and rug that you ignore. But when you suffer a real setback, you want to know all the reasons why—so that it will never happen again.

Essentially, I came to the realization that I was simply trying to do too much. Success brings a lot of different things with it. Many of those things are terrific, but some of them aren't. Some of them force us away from what we originally set out to do. I originally set out to be a coach. But every year it seemed to get harder and harder just to get the chance to coach my team.

We were achieving like crazy. Because we went to five straight Final Fours and won two national championships, I found myself confronted with an extreme. In this case, it was extreme success. And you have to be careful when you're dealing with extremes. They throw you out of your normal rhythm and, sometimes, you begin to think of only yourself.

I found myself saying, "I've got to do this again. I've got to go to the Final Four again. I've got to win the national championship again."

Well, there's that singular pronoun—"I." And I had always coached with the maxim that plural pronouns should be the norm.

Not only that, but that train I'm always talking about just got too full. We never had a chance to stop the "Success Express" to enjoy our journey. And as the conductor on the train, it was wearing me down most of all.

All the achievements resulted in hundreds of requests to participate in causes—almost all of them noble and worthwhile. We used to receive thirty letters a week—now we were getting bins of letters. People wanted me to speak at their luncheons. "We need you to be on this committee for USA Basketball." "We need you to help out with the National Association of Basketball Coaches." "Coach K, we're having a big fund-raiser. Can you be a part of it?"

Well, the year is not a thousand days. I simply did not have time to do all of the things that were requested of me.

But I tried to. I tried to do everything. That was part of my problem.

I think it gets back to the fact that I'm from Augusta Boulevard in Chicago. Because I achieved all this success, I felt I had to give something back. And then, when I did get involved with something, I was like a crusader. I care. So I do the very best I can.

A number of people have speculated that my problem was due to the fact that "Coach K got his priorities out of whack." Well, I don't think that's true. Over the past thirty years, if anyone asked me what my priorities were, I'd list them in perfect order the same way every time.

I believe, rather, that the time I devoted to those priorities got out of whack. I became so busy that I wasn't managing my time wisely. I couldn't believe it but, as I thought things through, one of the major lessons I learned was to manage my time more wisely.

Time management is one of the first principles we teach our kids when they come to Duke during the preseason. And if I teach it, I'd better be able to do it myself.

Another key lesson learned is that once leaders experience a certain amount of success, they need people around who will say no for them—especially if the success involves a substantial amount of media attention. When we were winning championships on a regular basis, I became more than a coach, I became an idea.

"Hey, let's get Coach K to do this. We'll raise $50,000 by putting on a special event and getting him to take the lead." "What a great idea, let's ask him."

Well, if someone comes to me with their great idea and I

have to say no to them, it doesn't exactly lead to a great situation. As a matter of fact, I go from being loved to being hated in a matter of moments—and I didn't even do anything except decline.

"What a jerk that Coach K is! He's changed. He's not the guy I thought he was. Success has gone to his head. Can you believe it? He can't do this one little thing?"

Many of my requests are now screened by Mike Cragg, Duke's sports information director, and Gerry Brown, my executive assistant. Both are aware of my schedule so they can immediately say no if I'm tied up. And they also are able to make recommendations on the really important requests that should be considered most seriously.

At first, Gerry was apprehensive about making some of those decisions for me. She didn't want to make a mistake that might harm me. But she had more trouble accepting mistakes than I did. So Mickie told her that she had a good enough relationship with me that, almost all of the time, her judgment would be correct. And even if it wasn't, she should go ahead and make a mistake once in a while. Gerry could learn as she went along—and we would all still be better off.

Of course, we don't always say no to appeals for help. A variety of people from good causes ask me to help and I feel compelled to honor as many requests as is reasonable.

Personally, I've always had a soft spot for anything that has to do with kids. As a matter of fact, whenever our team is feeling a little bit blue about a loss, I'll take some of the players over to the Duke Medical Center to visit with the kids. Right away, we get our perspective back. Our team members will also visit schools around the community to advise young people to read and stay away from drugs.

And Mickie and I, personally, do a lot for the Duke Children's Hospital. For instance, we chair the national advisory board for the hospital and, for fifteen years, we've chaired the Children's Miracle Network. I also do a lot of work for the Cancer Comprehensive Center, Coaches vs. Cancer, and I'm on the board of directors for the Jimmy V Foundation, to name a few. I try to put in as much time as I can with these great organizations and, believe me, I've gotten much more back than I have put in.

Along with achieving a certain amount of fame and success comes a powerful forum to influence others. And I believe people who find themselves in that situation have the responsibility to use that power wisely. We also have the responsibility to help people whenever we can, to provide a flicker of hope to someone who may be having a tough time, and to demonstrate with our actions that love and compassion are not meaningless or hollow words.

I receive thousands of letters every year from people all around the world. Many are from Duke basketball fans who express well wishes and appreciation for our success. But most are from people who have been touched by something other than winning basketball games. Let me mention a few examples:

One note came from the grandfather of a young boy fighting cancer who had gone through chemotherapy, losing his hair and, possibly worst of all for him, having to restrict his activities. We arranged for tickets to a game for the entire family and sent a letter of encouragement. "Never once did I hear him complain," wrote the grandfather. "From the bottom of my heart, thanks for your kindnesses to my grandson and to all the many other kids you must also touch."

Another letter came from a twelve-year-old boy who saw an interview I did on ESPN about the Jimmy V Foundation. "I was very touched and wanted to donate some of my paper route money," he wrote. "I know this is not a lot of money, but it comes from my heart. Could you please give it to someone special with cancer or to the Mr. Jimmy V Foundation. I wish I could do more in life. I would like to help someone."

And one year I received a note from a former player I had coached back in the early 1970s. It seemed that he had recently received a double-lung transplant and was told by his doctors that the main reason he survived was due to his will and determination. Then he credited me for instilling that quality in him at a young age. He reminded me that I once put him in a game with a huge lead and he immediately took an ill-advised jump shot from the top of the key. I quickly yanked him and told him that his best attribute was in passing. Then, during the last game of the season, I put him back in the lineup at the end of a game in which we had a large lead. He took a charge from the opponent's big power forward and slid several feet on his rear. And then I praised him up one side and down the other. It was one of those small acts of courage on the basketball court that I admire—and I told the player I admired him for it. "All I want for you to know is that you made a huge difference in my life," he wrote in his letter, "and I apologize that it has taken me twenty-five years to say thank you."

People send me letters like these because they care.

And I care, too. That's why, with the help of our staff, I try to answer every single letter that comes my way.

I often will share these letters with members of our team —so they can keep life in perspective, so they can know how they might affect people if they do the right and noble thing.

And since my return to coaching full-time, I also share the lessons I've learned with our players.

Don't try to do too much yourself.

Remember, it's "we" not "I."

Stop the "Success Express" every now and then to enjoy the journey.

Manage your time wisely.

If you're inundated with requests that impact your time, we have people who will say no for you—so no one will think you're a jerk.

If you get too many fan letters and don't have time to answer them all, our staff will help you. We're set up to take care of it now.

Can you help with the hospital, with the kids? Well, of course you can. Just be sure and take care of yourself first.

Remember Your Core

While I sat out the season, our team fell apart and we finished with a 13-18 record. So upon my return, I had to build the program back up again—hopefully, to where it had once been. In order for me to do that, I had to accept the fact that the team had deteriorated because I had allowed us to get away from our core. Heck, I had actually deteriorated *physically* because I got away from my own core.

Sometimes in our haste to accomplish, we forget why we're doing it. The truth is that I had violated the basic premises that originally allowed us to achieve all our success. Now I had to get back to them.

I pulled out the videotape of Quin Snyder's senior speech and I wrote down those words he mentioned: commitment, integrity, toughness, honesty, collective responsibility, pride, love, and friendship. I placed the list in my notebook and car-

ried it around with me. And I vowed to myself that we, as a

team, would get back to the core principles on that list—because that's what made us go. It certainly is what made me go. Getting back to those things would then lead to winning the ACC regular season, winning the tournament, going to the Big Dance, going to the Final Four.

I also thought back to the earlier days of my coaching career—even all the way back to when I was a kid in Chicago. I remembered that we didn't have organized leagues, that we didn't get trophies for winning. We just played the game.

We played because we enjoyed it. We played because we were friends. We played for innocence.

Then I realized, once again, that those basketball games were the vehicle for my relationships with my friends. And now, as an adult, coaching basketball is still my vehicle for relationships and friendships. In fact, coaching basketball is my vehicle for life itself—for the larger journey.

If the only reason I coached was to win college basketball games, my life would be pretty shallow. I coach not only because I love it, but because I have the chance to teach and interact with young people.

At the end of every season, I don't think so much about the number of games we won or how far we got on the road to the national championship. Rather, I think about all the kids on the team and what we lived through together that year. I think about Chris Collins, Tony Lang, Jeff Capel, Cherokee Parks, Jay Bilas, and the scores of other guys who've played on our teams over the years. When I see one of them, whether it's in person or on television, I smile. I know I've impacted their lives. And they have certainly impacted mine for the better.

And you know what?

Because of that view of life, because of those relationships, I have no baggage. I don't lie awake at night thinking about the national championship games we did not win. I don't define my life by how many games we've won—or by the dictum "I scored more than you."

Since I came back from my season out, I constantly ask myself the question: "What's your job, knucklehead?"

Answer: "I'm the Duke basketball coach. My job is to be the leader of my basketball program. My job is to be the husband and father of my family. Do your job, Mike. Do your job."

A person has to take care of his core. And my core revolves around my family and coaching basketball. It always has. In fact, I'm probably the only Columbo from the old neighborhood in Chicago who's doing right now what I wanted to do when I was nine years old. I'm a lucky guy. I'm living my dream. And in my case, reality is better than the dream itself.

Today, I try to keep a balance with all the people and things I love in my life.

There are many games to be played and, hopefully, they're not just basketball games. There are dances to be danced, pianos to be played, and cheers to be cheered. I want to play those games, too. I don't want to be one-dimensional and have my whole life revolve around a series of screens and picks to produce a basket.

It's funny, but out of the dark days of that season came light and renewal. It was good to know that I was mortal. When life goes wrong for us, as it sometimes does, we just have to figure out what we can do better the next time around.

For me, it was not a season lost, it was a season found.

The year I came back, the 1995–1996 season, was perhaps my most critical year in coaching. We were coming off a disastrous losing season, we had a fragile team, and the players were lacking confidence in themselves. I felt the team really needed to make the NCAA tournament to show that we had turned things around.

By mid-February, however, it was looking pretty bleak—especially after a loss to Wake Forest put our record at 4-7 in conference play. I was certain we had to finish with at least an 8-8 record in order to get an invitation to the tournament. We had five ACC games remaining and I knew we were only headed in one direction as a team—and that was down.

I assembled the staff together and explained that we had pushed this team as far as it could go. "Guys, if we don't do something right now, we're not going to make the tournament," I told them. "It's obvious to me that I have to do something with Chris Collins. We'll have to follow his heart from here on out."

Chris was a senior that year. He was our captain, our leader, our core. The previous season, he had broken his foot—and this year, he was playing with a pin in it. All the players, to a man, respected his tenacity and his courage.

So after practice, I took Chris aside and we watched some videotapes and discussed ways he could improve. Then I turned off the tape and we had a quiet moment together, just the two of us.

"Look, Chris, I'm going to ask you to do something," I said. "For the rest of the season, I want you to play without thinking. I want you to follow your instincts. If you've got a shot when you come across half-court, I want you to take it. If you see an opening for a drive to the basket, take it. I want you to play where there are no restrictions. Don't be afraid to fail. Act like it's impossible to fail.

"Now, I'm not going to mention this to the rest of the team. Anything you do, Chris, will be okay—and I'll cover your 275 back. But from here on out, we win or we lose with you. Is that too much pressure?"

"No," he replied.

"But do you understand? I'm saying that you can do anything—anything!"

"I understand, Coach. I'll do it."

Over the next five games, all of which we won, Chris Collins played like a man possessed. He had 23 points against Virginia, 12 points against NC State, 27 points against Florida State, 27 points against UCLA, and another 27-point game against Maryland.

He was simply amazing. During the Florida State game, we were behind in the last few minutes and he came down and popped in a couple of three-pointers from well behind the three-point line. And I could hear people in the crowd behind me wonder aloud what had gotten into Chris Collins. "How's he shooting that ball? He just barely got over half-court on that last one!"

In our final game against North Carolina, Chris had 18 points in the first 25 minutes of play—and then he reinjured his foot and I had to take him out. But even though we lost that last game, we achieved an 8-8 conference record and secured an invitation to the Big Dance.

The next week, we lost in the first round of the NCAA tournament to a talented Eastern Michigan team. And when the game was over, Chris Collins was limping in pain and crying. His tears were not caused by the injury or because we had lost, but because he had played his last game in a Duke uniform—and because he had given it his all.

When he came to the bench, I put my arms around him and hugged him.

"I love you, Chris," I said. "Thank you. Thank you."

The previous year, when I was out, we finished with a 13-18 record. That year, we were 18-13. And the difference was the heart of Chris Collins.

Chris was a bridge to greatness for Duke basketball. He put passion and guts and inspiration back into our team. His heart led us into the NCAA tournament that year and helped us win the league championship the very next season. Because, even though he had graduated, two underclassmen on Chris's team had taken particular notice of the example he set.

Steve Wojciechowski and Trajan Langdon had watched and learned. And, subsequently, they were able to take the lead themselves.

Coach K's Tips

- Sometimes, when you're blinded by your emotions and your commitments, it's best for someone else to tell you what to do.

- Once in a while, you have to be committed to yourself—and yourself only.

- People look at things closer when they lose than when they win.

- Be careful when you're dealing with extremes. They throw you off your normal rhythm and you begin to use singular pronouns like "I."

- Stop the "Success Express" once in a while to enjoy the journey.

- If you teach it, you better be able to do it yourself.

- Have people around who will say no for you.

- When things go wrong for you and your team, assume responsibility. Admit your mistakes and move on.

- Regularly ask yourself the question: "What's your job, knucklehead?"

- Take care of your core.

- Listen to your doctors.

EPILOGUE

"I think of my mom every day of my life."

—**Coach K**

One day in early 1995, just before I took the rest of the season off, I was sitting in my office reviewing videotapes of an upcoming opponent when I received a phone call from my mom.

"Hi, Mike," she said. "I don't want to bother you or take up too much of your time."

"No, Mom," I said, "you can bother me every second of every day. When have you ever bothered me?"

I don't remember the rest of the conversation. What I do remember is that, after I hung up the phone, I cried.

"You stupid idiot," I said to myself. "Your mom's eighty-three years old. How can she feel that way?"

As observant as I am about people, I wasn't observant about myself. I didn't spend enough time with the people who loved me the most. I was so into achieving that I was driving them away. I was alone. It was stupid of me.

So here I was, approaching age fifty, and my mom had taught me one of life's most valuable lessons. And she didn't need a whole team to get my attention. Rather than telling me I wasn't taking enough time for my family, she simply used the word "bother." I don't want to "bother" you.

Jimmy Valvano had tried to tell me the same thing just before he died. "Don't screw it up, Mike," he said.

Well, I had screwed it up. But now, I knew better. And, besides, my mom didn't raise a dummy. I know it'll never happen again. And now, when our team is participating in a tournament, I'll get everybody together after the game in our hotel room and I'll look them in the eyes. (Don't forget: If you always look in your players' eyes—whether it's victory or defeat—you're going to get the most out of your profession.)

"Okay, guys," I'll say, "here's your schedule for tomorrow. Now, you're going to get hit by autograph seekers and all that. But don't spend time with them until you have acknowledged the important people in your life. You go right to your mother and give her a hug. If your mom is not here, go call her. Share the moment with her—or your father, or whoever is important in your life. Now go be with your families."

That was a huge lesson to learn—huge. I felt lucky to have my mom do that for me. Because from that point on, I have never forgotten that I need to spend most of my time with the people who count most in my life—my family.

It's also poignant, I think, that it was my mom who got that message across to me, because it was one of the last things she did for me. Not too long after that, I received a phone call from my brother, Bill. It was one of those calls that every son or daughter knows will come sooner or later, but hopes never to have to take. My mom, who had been suffering from cancer, was failing quickly now.

I hopped on a plane to Chicago and flew to her bedside. I was lucky. I got to spend the last week with her. She slept most of the time, but when she was awake, we talked, we laughed, we cried.

While I was there, I tried to will the cancer out of her. I never believed it would get the best of her. But it did. And now there's a hole in my heart that can never be filled.

I think of my mom every day of my life. She was as happy a person as I've ever been around. She made fun of herself and was telling jokes until the day she died—literally. She never had much money. No cars. She didn't have a house. But she was happy. She led a great life. She was proud. And people loved her. Tell me that's not success.

When we are young and growing up, we tend to take our parents for granted. We don't think of telling them how much we love them or how much they've meant to us. My father died when I was young. But, thank God, my mom lived long enough for me to tell her those things. And I didn't wait until her last day to do it.

About midway through my time at Duke, she was spending a few weeks with us in Durham—helping us when we were putting on the summer basketball camp.

Well, one day, we were sitting on the porch together. Jamie was real little at the time and sitting in her lap.

"So, how are things going, Mike?"

"Good, Mom."

"How did it happen that you're the coach at Duke and you're on TV? How did that happen?" she asked out of the blue.

And I said, "It happened because of you."

"Mike! C'mon."

"It happened because of you, Mom. If I do my thing as well as you've lived your life, I'll be unbelievably successful."

"Mike! C'mon!"

"Mom, it's the truth. I could never be more committed to anything that I did, or to a person, than you were committed to Bill and me, to our family. No way. When people ask me where I learned commitment, I tell them I learned it from you. When they ask me about unconditional support, I learned it from you. Not being afraid to fail? From you.

"Mom, you know I love you. I know how much you've done for me. That's why all this has happened. And I want to thank you for it."

She paused and looked at me for a moment. And I believe I saw her eyes moisten before she broke the silence with one final "Mike! C'mon!"

A few weeks after my mom passed away, I received a package from my brother, Bill, who had been going through things in her apartment.

He had found a ledger that he felt I should have. It contained a list, written out in my mom's handwriting, of every game my teams had played while I was a head coach. It covered a period of twenty years—starting with my very first game at West Point and ending with the last game we had played at Duke. Each entry contained the date, the name of the opponent, the final score, and an L or a W. I never knew she was keeping that ledger.

Also in the package was my mother's rosary.

And now, before every game, I put her rosary in my shirt pocket so that it's close to my heart. And when our team is

283

warming up out on the court, when I'm all alone, I'll put my hand over my shirt pocket and say a prayer in honor of my mom. I ask God to look out after her. And I say:

"Please, God, help me do my best, help me be myself, and help me lead with my heart."

OVERTIME

FALL 2004

I still think of my mom every day of my life. When I was young, she was my strongest source of reassurance and support. I was also greatly influenced by the community center of the inner-city Polish neighborhood where I grew up. Durham, North Carolina, where I live now, has a similar neighborhood on its west end with a variety of nationalities and incomes. So it seemed a good idea for me to establish a community center there and name it in honor of my mom.

We designed the Emily Krzyzewski Family Life Center to be a place that touches the hopes and dreams of people of all ages—and then helps make those hopes and dreams a reality. Planning and fundraising went very well in the first few years and we broke ground for the new center in August 2003.

Not long after we made the announcement of the center's founding, however, there was a bit of a backlash from people involved with other community centers in the area. So we held a meeting with representatives from all the centers. We showed everybody our plans, said that we wanted to work together, and then formed a group to make sure that no toes were stepped on. Initially, I had not anticipated such a negative reaction. But after thinking about it awhile, I realized it was really a natural human reaction to change.

College Basketball's Changing Environment

Change is something with which I'm confronted more and more, especially in my profession. Over the last five years, college basketball has changed significantly and it continues to evolve at a rapid pace. Sometimes, I feel like I'm walking through an airport next to one of those moving walkways. The national college game is on the walkway and moving a lot quicker than I am. The reality is that I've got to walk faster, even run, to keep up. And if I don't find a way to get on the moving walkway in a hurry, it's going to leave me so far behind that I'll never be able to catch up.

What's changing about college basketball? Well, for one thing, it is becoming much more individualized. The beauty of our game is that it was founded on the premise of people working together and helping one another achieve a shared goal. That's what teamwork is all about. And basketball is truly a great team sport—loaded with plays like the pass, for instance, where one player "connects" with another. What's more, basketball has always been filled with plural pronouns. How do *we* look? What's the best thing for *us*? How can *our* team improve? Right now, though, the sport is in much more of a singular pronoun world than ever before. The lure of big money in the National Basketball Association has the media speculating whether or not a good player will leave his university early. Can *he* go pro? How high will *he* go in the draft? How much money will *he* make? Young college players then ask their coaches questions like, when do you think *I* will be ready to go pro? How much money will *I* be able to make? Sometimes, we're not even talking about a college education anymore! Yet that's really why they should be here in the first place. So now we have all the ingredients for an unusually selfish environment. But basketball is beautiful, in part, because it is unselfish.

In the five years since *Leading with the Heart* was first published, Duke basketball has done very well. We've won four Atlantic Coast Conference championships and gone to five NCAA Tournaments (advancing to five Sweet Sixteens, two Final Fours, and winning one national championship). Along the way, our program has been heavily affected by college basketball's changing environment. Let me give you a couple of examples.

For one thing, recruiting has changed significantly. Today, at high school basketball games, there are often more NBA representatives present than there are college coaches. And the professional scouts don't have to adhere to the same rules we do. We are not allowed, for instance, to speak with a coach, player, or parents—and we have to sit in specially designated sections of the stands. The pros, however, may talk to whomever they want and can sit wherever they wish.

NBA scouts may also recruit at any time. But college coaches are strictly limited. In May and June of 2004, there was a big high school tournament being conducted at the University of North Carolina, North Carolina State, and Duke. There were games being played in our own arena, Cameron Indoor Stadium, but NCAA recruiting rules prohibited us from watching them. NBA scouts could be there, though. And of course, when the students see the logos of the Knicks, the Lakers, the Spurs, and the other teams, it just naturally influences them. That impact lasts well into their college careers if they do not choose to go pro right out of high school. When you think about it, we really cannot compete with the NBA's brand. As a result, college basketball is, in my opinion, losing its own brand.

At the end of a season, if we unexpectedly lose one or more players to the NBA, it is not possible for us to make up for the loss. NCAA recruiting rules will not allow us to fill those voids. This is exactly what happened to us at the close of the 2004 season.

Our team that year, although not loaded with an abundance of individual talent, really came together as a team. But right after our appearance in the 2004 Final Four, the "Fist" flexed open and we suddenly went from being a team to being a group of individuals. Our star freshman, Luol Deng, announced that he was going to enter the NBA draft. And Shawn Livingston, a high school recruit who had been committed to us for more than a year, informed us that he, too, was considering going pro. With Luol and Shawn on our team, I'm fairly certain Duke would have been among the top picks in the preseason polls and a favorite to win the 2005 national championship. As it turned out, we were looking at not only losing Chris Duhon, our senior leader, but also at having only eight scholarship players as opposed to ten. It put us in a very tough and, of course, unplanned situation.

I'm not sure we can achieve success in the same manner we did when we won the 2001 national championship. All this change has really affected the family atmosphere we've created at Duke. In a way, I think it mirrors our society in that it is more difficult to keep a family together now than it was two decades ago.

When we had teams with freshmen, sophomores, juniors, and seniors, we were more balanced, more spread out in a good way. It allowed us to have many teachers and leaders. As a result, we were able to build stronger bonds of trust, communicate more effectively, and instill higher levels of confidence in all our players. The older guys formed strong relationships with the younger ones. They were like big and little brothers. That's why Quin Snyder will always be close with Johnny Dawkins, Chris Collins with Grant Hill, and Chris Duhon with Shane Battier. That kind of family culture, that maturation process, gave a lot back to our organization.

But now we're losing those "older brothers." We can no longer count on having a senior for the others to look up to. Great players lead by example—by their work ethic, their sacrifices, and how they conduct themselves on a daily basis. They inspire greatness in those around them.

A Leader Has to Find a Way to Win

In business terms, I guess you could say that the changes in our environment have been causing us to receive less of a return on our investment. Obviously, we're getting less of a return with points and rebounds because our players are, on average, not staying a full four years. But we also receive less of a return in what they give back to the team.

Still, though, Duke has won 152 games (most in the nation) over the past five years, including 16 wins in the NCAA Tournament (also most in the nation). We've been ranked number one in the national polls at some point during each of those five years. For three of the last six years, we have finished the season with the top RPI rating in college basketball. We've been a #1 seed in the NCAA Tournament four of the last five years. And recently, somebody told me about a statistic that I had not yet heard. Apparently, in my twenty-four years at Duke, I've coached more games when our teams were number one in the country than I've coached when we were unranked.

The reason I mention all this is that businesspeople are always asking me about how Duke basketball consistently remains competitive. "How do you stay number one when your environment is changing so rapidly?" I'm asked. Well, the answer is really fairly simple. You have a choice. You can either change with the environment or you will eventually fail. A leader has to find a way to win.

The question is not whether or not you should change. The question is *how* you should change. *What* should you do? In our case, there was no established road map to follow because changes of this kind had never happened before. I couldn't go to an older coach and ask: "What did you do when this happened to you?" Our basketball program was in uncharted waters. So we've had to work harder, better, and in different ways. In some respects, it's trial and error. But a leader can never stop and say: "Aha! Here's a failsafe way to do it!" Baloney! There is no failsafe way of doing things—no magic formula, no perfect recipe.

In attempting new things and adjusting to change, however, we must not lower our standards. The basic values upon which we build our program—such as getting our students an education and teaching excellence, family, and character—do not change. Neither does the basic concept of teamwork or teaching the elements of the Fist (communication, trust, collective responsibility, caring, and pride).

With these important principles remaining inflexible at Duke, we began transforming our culture to meet the larger changing environment. Over the last five years, we focused on three main areas: relationships, building trust face-to-face, and exerting more direct control.

Relationships

Because we're almost certain to lose players in less than four years, we attempt to build relationships with our students earlier and more in-depth than ever before. First of all, we spend a lot more time talking with potential recruits about things other than basketball. We used to think that every kid we signed up did not have to be a leader. Now we strategically search for high school juniors and rising seniors who have demonstrated leadership on their teams. We look for students who have the ability to care about what their teammates are doing, who see the bigger picture, who show a propensity to think and act outside of themselves. Many are captains of their teams or have some significant outside interests that distinguish them. By recruiting high school players with leadership skills, we have a better chance of seeing them become leaders on the court when they are underclassmen.

We also know that just about every player we have wants to play professional basketball, whether in the NBA or in Europe. So we acknowledge that from the beginning and try to help them achieve that goal. "Let us help you get there," we'll tell them. "Let us advise and work with you. We've done it before with players like Jason Williams and Carlos Boozer, for example." Rather than trying to bind our students to a four-year deal, we now work with them on a year-to-year basis. But we also advise them not to set a time limit on their tenure at Duke. We ask them to unpack their bags. "You are not at an extended stay motel," we'll say. "Make this a home. Throw yourself into it. Each person has his own race. Elton Brand had his and it went two years. Shane Battier had his and it went four. Both were national players of the year and both played on the same team."

Another thing we attempt to do is bring our signed recruits into the fold earlier so they'll more quickly feel part of the team. Of course, that's not as easy as it might sound because of the NCAA restricted environment in which we operate. We are not allowed, for instance, to place phone calls to high school juniors—and we can only call seniors an average of once a week. Therefore, I have to plan ahead in order to make every conversation worthwhile. When calling a recruit, I may discuss more than just who won a recent Duke game or by how many points. Or I may point out that our coaches are working with a particular player about a confidence issue. "This is the kind of thing you may go through next year," I'll say. "What would you do?" Or I might point out, "This might be happening on your current team. Why don't you partner with your coach? That's what you'll need to do when you get here." I never did that before the college basketball environment changed so radically. I didn't have to.

Building Trust Face-to-Face

One of the biggest changes in our program is the fact that we no longer have as many upperclassmen around to teach the younger players. In the past, I would ask a leader like Shane Battier to talk to the underclassmen about certain key points. And he would say things to them like: "Hey, you just don't do that. Here's how. Here's why. Let me show you what Coach K meant." And often Shane would do so without me ever asking him. It was a lot easier for me to develop trust among the team when I had a senior leader hanging on my every word and then taking action on his own initiative. How do you replace that?

Time is needed to develop deep relationships. When we had players staying for the full four years, we were able to build a very high level of trust because every year added on to the previous one. But all that has changed. We now have to forge strong bonds in a shorter period of time. It's like a builder of custom homes who normally takes a year to build his best house. Then, all of a sudden, he's told that he has to build the same quality house in only six months. And he has to do it with a younger, less seasoned crew.

That brings up a couple of interesting questions. How does a leader continue to build trust when he doesn't have senior experience around anymore? How do you develop just as much trust in only three years, two years, one year?

In my opinion, leadership relies very heavily on face-to-face communication—especially in the areas of building relationships and establishing trust. Accordingly, our coaching staff has strategically increased the amount of personal time we spend with our players. Having three former players with me as assistant coaches is even more valuable to our program now. Johnny Dawkins, Steve Wojciechowski, and Chris Collins spent four years in the Duke program. They were all leaders in their own right. They discuss, guide, and share more of their own experiences when they were students playing the game. In a way, they now act as the seniors (or the big brothers) we lack.

Johnny Dawkins, for example, leads our new year-round player development program where every player is reached on a weekly basis. He and our staff will buddy-up with the players. They'll schedule meetings and discussions. They'll call the players on the phone regularly—during the summer months as well as the regular school year. "Hey, how are you doing today? What's going on?" In addition to building better relationships, it shows that we care about them. And it provides a vehicle for us to both give and receive feedback. By having the students interact more regularly with our younger assistant coaches, they are more likely to speak up if something is on their mind. And being closer to their age than I am, Johnny, Wojo, or Chris might be able to explain something so they more easily understand it. The staff's increased involvement also inspires their taking more ownership of the team. They care for the players to a higher degree—a degree that can only be achieved through the forging of deep personal bonds.

As head coach, I also provide more one-on-one contact than I used to—and not just in terms of basketball. During the 2004 season, I conducted an informal leadership class with four of our players—a senior (Chris Duhon), a junior (Daniel Ewing), a sophomore (J. J. Redick), and a freshman, (Luol Deng). I would have them read chapters of *Leading with the Heart*. Then we would meet regularly and talk. We not only became closer to each other, but I believe it helped our team get to the Final Four.

Exerting More Direct Control

A big result of college basketball's changing environment is the fact that younger players are now thrown into leadership roles before they're ready. During a game, I can call a play for a younger team, and they may run it just as flawlessly as they did in practice. But if the opposing defense throws a twist at them, something that is unexpected, they have a tendency to freeze up. "Uh oh!" they may think. "Can't run the play over there. What do we do now?"

On the other hand, a more veteran team will react spontaneously and score anyway. They'll look for a hole in the defense or some sort of opening in which to operate. And if they see an opportunity, they'll make a play. It might not be the one I called in the first place, but they will still score. And that's exactly what I want them to do. I want them to take action on their own in order to get the job done. Any play I call for them should be viewed as nothing more than a base upon which to operate.

Part of leadership is simply the ability to react spontaneously in order to make plays in a changing environment. It takes time, however, to develop that ability. Freshmen and sophomores are usually too young to act with such spontaneity. They lack the confidence that comes from experience. But as a senior, Christian Laettner had no problem saying: "Just give me the ball." Grant Hill and Shane Battier would simply grab the ball and make big plays. Veteran players realize they don't always have to ask for permission to do things. They can just act.

Because our players often lack such key experience, our coaching staff now has to exert more direct control over the team. At times, it can be a delicate balance—encouraging them to take initiative, but also telling them specifically what to do. During games, for instance, we encourage our players to shoot frequently. But we also call more plays for them. In a crucial game situation, I might call a timeout and say, "Okay, now is the time for you to do what we've worked on in practice!" When the head coach takes control of a situation like that, it tends to give a less-experienced team more confidence.

It seems to help them believe that they can, in fact, successfully execute the play.

The same thing goes for class work. If we guide the students properly in their studies, they'll become confident they can obtain a degree. While we are not allowed to work with them specifically on basketball during certain periods of the year, we can indoctrinate them into the college system.

So we bring in our new recruits the summer before their freshman year as part of a three-pronged approach designed to give them a solid base upon which to build. 1) We focus on *academics* to help them get off to a good start in their class work; 2) We help them *socially* so that they may better adjust to their new environment and being away from home; and 3) *athletically*, we start them on an intense physical workout schedule that helps them bridge the gap from high school to college. (Due to NCAA restrictions, we are not allowed to work with them on basketball skills).

Regarding academics, our new recruits take two courses that first summer. Then after their first full year, in which they can get eight other courses under their belts, we bring them in for the next session of summer school, where they may take an additional two courses. Consequently, after that second summer, our rising sophomores may already have earned as many as twelve credits—which is one-third of what they need to obtain their degrees. That way, if they leave early, they have a better chance to graduate.

I try to never forget that our players are students first and basketball players second. If we were just trying to develop their basketball talents alone, we'd be shortchanging them. Moreover, bringing them into the fold sooner helps our athletic program. By the time the students officially start the regular school year, they've already learned the new things that freshmen have to learn. And to top it all off, we have already established a personal relationship with each of them.

During the 2003 season, after we lost three key players to the NBA, our team had six freshmen on it. As a result, our coaching staff was forced to virtually recreate our entire culture. But that turned out to be a good thing. It made us re-evaluate our situation, think in more depth, and change accordingly. It also brought us closer together—closer, I think, than we had ever been. We threw away the organizational chart and made some significant changes that year. We all did what we had to do. We did what made sense. And then, as we progressed through the next couple of years, we constantly adjusted our methods to achieve better results.

Some of the changes we implemented were things we should have been doing all along. So in the end, trying to find different ways to win made us all better leaders.

Chris Duhon

It's difficult to see our younger players leave early for the NBA. Of much more concern than their not playing basketball for us is the fact that we're not able to continue close relationships with them for another year or two. For me, it's like losing a friend. But there are still great players here for the full four years to make it all worthwhile. Chris Duhon was one of those players.

As a freshman on our 2001 national championship team, Chris was significantly influenced by the leadership of seniors Shane Battier and Nate James. But just a few years later, in 2003, he was a junior trying to carry six freshmen on his shoulders. And there were a lot of high expectations. As a matter of

297

fact, he was one of the preseason favorites to be named national player of the year. Actually, Chris Duhon was the first younger player to feel the impact of all these guys leaving early for the NBA. When Elton Brand and two others left in 1999, Shane Battier still had Nate James. But in 2003, Duhon was all alone.

All this placed a lot of stress on Chris. As a result, he did not have as good a year as everyone expected. He simply couldn't do everything that needed to be done. He put too much pressure on himself to assume the mantle of leadership and he just wasn't ready. Even though we won twenty-six games and made it to the Sweet Sixteen, a lot of people were down on him. Chris had tried so hard to lead that his play on the court suffered. As a result, he lost confidence in himself.

Over the summer, our coaching staff spent a lot of extra time with Chris. We talked about leadership on and off the court—both privately and in our unofficial discussions surrounding *Leading with the Heart* (together with Daniel, J. J., and Luol). We gave him a lot of thought-provoking, inspirational assignments to read. And then we would get together and discuss them. What does it mean to be committed? How are we going to look out for one another? We talked about a lot of things like that in much more detail and more often. We had him speak with guidance counselors. And we worked closely with Chris's mom, Vivian Harper. We trusted her and she trusted us to do the very best for her son. She was pivotal in Chris's development.

Creating a great team takes more than one year. It isn't like making a cake, putting it in the oven for forty-five minutes, and then "presto" it's done. It has to bake longer. You have to keep it in the oven. Actually, it may take two or three full seasons to forge a championship team. We used the 2003 season to build upon and, in 2004, things started to gel. As the Fist started coming together, Chris Duhon became the story of the season. He turned out to be an extension of me on the court. He brought everybody together. And like all great leaders, he made some big spontaneous plays when it really counted.

For example, with thirty-six seconds to play in a close home game against Florida State, Duhon made a clutch three-point shot when everybody else on our team was afraid to shoot. I didn't call that play from the bench. The play I called was designed to have J. J. Redick or Daniel Ewing take the shot. But Florida State's defense prevented an easy execution of the play—so Chris instinctively seized the moment, made a big play, and won the game for us.

A week later, on North Carolina's home court, with the game tied and ten seconds left in overtime, Chris gave us the win by taking an inbounds pass under our own basket, dribbling the length of the court, weaving through a maze of players, and then delivering a beautiful reverse layup a few seconds before time expired.

Chris Duhon was also the story of the NCAA tournament. A week earlier, he had received a severe rib injury in the ACC tournament championship game against Maryland. Moving at full speed, Chris dove for a loose ball out of bounds. He slid across the floor and hit the metal base of a TV camera stand. A hush quickly came over the crowd. After being down for several minutes, he was taken into the locker room for an examination. Nobody knew if he was going to be coming back or not. But after being cleared by the doctors, Chris ran back onto the court and came right up to me.

"I'm ready, coach," he said.

He then went into the game on his own, played valiantly, and almost helped us pull out a win. Chris Duhon did what you would expect a senior leader to do. No excuses. Next play. What can I do to help the team? I'm ready to go.

Subsequently, during the first couple of weeks of the Big Dance, Chris was unable to practice and he became *the* big media story. "Will Duhon be ready to play?" "Will the pain be too much for him?" "Will Duke be without the services of its leader?" Well, Duhon did play. In fact, he had the most minutes on the court of anybody on our team. In nearly thirty years of coaching, I've never had a student play with more pain. And despite the pain, Chris had one of the best defensive games of his career during our regional championship victory. Our opponent, Xavier, had two hot shooters and I assigned him to alternately guard each of them. Whichever guy he was on at that moment became a cold shooter. Defense played a big part in that championship game. And with the win, we advanced to the Final Four.

Through it all, there was no gloom and doom from Chris. "Coach, I can handle the pain," he'd say. "I can play. I'll be there." Chris served as an example for our team. His strength inspired the other players—and it inspired me. He led us to thirty-one victories and a Final Four appearance. We got that far because of Chris Duhon's heart. He gave us a chance to win. There's no doubt about it.

As unselfish a player as he was, Chris also put up some glowing personal statistics. He completed his career as the only player in ACC history to have more than 1,000 points, 800 assists, 400 rebounds, and 300 steals. He is now Duke's all-time steals leader with 301 and is second all-time in assists with 819 (behind only NCAA record holder Bobby Hurley). He was named All-America and a finalist for 2004 national player of the year. And he was involved in 123 wins at Duke—second most by a player in ACC history. Chris Duhon's story shows just how much someone really can develop when he goes the full four years—not only as a basketball player, but as a leader, and as a person.

In the locker room after our final game of the season, Chris and I hugged each other in silence for several minutes. Both of us cried. Here was a young man who had given his whole heart to our team for all four years. We didn't say anything for the longest time. Finally I spoke. "Nobody has done more," I said. "Nobody has given us more. And I'll never forget that."

"I love you, Coach," he replied.

Chris didn't say anything else. He didn't have to.

Something Higher

During the summer of 2004, I held a team meeting to talk about unity. "Let's be men," I said to the players. "Let's move on. We need to help each other."

As a result of that meeting, one of our rising juniors, Shelden Williams, left a note on my desk. I was away at the time, but when I returned, someone said, "Shelden wants to see you."

Well, I must admit that my first reaction was "What's wrong now?" I was expecting him to say, "Here's something I want" or "Why is this happening to me?" You know—all those singular pronouns. I called him right away—before I noticed the note.

"Is something wrong, Shelden?" I asked.

"No, Coach. There's nothing wrong," he replied, "A lot of people think we're not going to be very good because we've had a few guys leave for the NBA. Well, we are going to be good. The note I left you just lists a few ideas I have for next year."

Upon hearing that, I broke into a big smile. Shelden was talking about "us." He was thinking ahead.

"You know, Coach," he continued, "as a freshman and sophomore, I just didn't feel as comfortable stepping forward to say things."

"Well, I'm glad you do now," I responded.

Sheldon then came over to my office. We had a nice long talk and our relationship went to the next level. I had similar conversations with some of the other players. And they really picked me up. It was like receiving a shot of adrenaline.

You know, a leader doesn't have to be the only person doing the inspiring. Sometimes we can draw inspiration from the members of our team. And leaders need that. In addition to all the pressures that come with shouldering the responsibilities of leadership, it can be a very lonely job if you let it.

I am frequently asked how leaders can balance everything in their lives. How do I keep going at such a fast pace, day in and day out, year in and year out? How do I balance my personal with my professional life? Well, for one thing, I try to stay in good physical condition. After two hip replacements and a back operation, I've had to adopt a new, less strenuous regimen. I try to exercise every day—but where I used to play basketball and run, I now engage in fast walking, weight training, and a variety of stretching exercises. I also play racquetball twice a week because I still want that competitive feeling (which is something I've been doing my entire life). By staying in good physical condition, I find I not only have more energy, but I also tend to have a more positive outlook on things.

Another thing I do to balance my personal and professional lives is to try to stay involved in a variety of outside interests. I believe getting involved can keep you grounded. Leaders tend to become isolated and spend too much time in the ivory tower. If that happens, they lose touch with their own people. On a higher level, leadership is all about understanding people—all people. And you can learn more about human nature by simply being involved in a variety of organizations.

A year ago, we established a center for organizational leadership and ethics at Duke's Fuqua School of Business, where I was honored to be named an executive-in-residence. I not only give several guest lectures during the year, but I'm also now part of a team that helps devise coursework and training in the field of leadership. One of the reasons I'm involved with this project is that I want to learn. By teaming up with the university, I'm able to be exposed to leaders in business through our yearly leadership conference. And that's invigorating. It's like a laboratory. I get to experiment with my own leadership style and try to find out if there's a better way.

I am also involved with a variety of charitable organizations. For me, it's a way of giving something back to society, of utilizing my platform to do good things. I serve on the board of the The Jimmy V Foundation, for instance, and continue to help with the Duke Children's Hospital, the Duke Cancer Comprehensive Center, the Brain Tumor Clinic, and a variety of other activities on campus and in the community. I believe it's important to give some of my personal time. After all, that's what I'm always asking the members of my team to do— to give some of their personal time for the betterment of the group, to get outside of themselves in different areas, and so on. As far as leadership goes, I think it's about setting a good example. It's about practicing what you preach.

The Emily Krzyzewski Family Life Center, especially, is a big focus for me right now—not only because it's named in honor of my mom, but because it's going to be an important institution in our local community. We'll have youth programs, adult programs, community help programs, and education programs—all tailored to the needs of local residents, all geared toward bringing people together. I hope the center will help a lot of people in Durham, just like the community center on the north side of Chicago helped me and so many others when I was growing up.

Interestingly enough, becoming as involved as I am with the project has also helped me discover something about myself. And it's made me a better leader. When we experienced the initial negative reaction to our plans for the center, I learned that I was viewed by some people in my own community as being somewhat intimidating.

I never really thought much about that before—and it caused me to reflect. As time passed and I became more successful, some people began to view me as unreachable, even intimidating. I had always thought of myself as being the same person, but perhaps who *I thought I was* and who *I was seen to be* were two different things.

So standing outside of myself for a moment, I came to the realization that I might actually be intimidating to my own players, especially the younger ones. It was ironic in a way. By achieving success, I had ended up distancing myself from the team—but a team is what I was trying to form.

Many leaders seem to get stale. They don't try to bridge the gap between the stature they have attained and the hopes and dreams of the people in their organizations. Rather than getting out of the ivory tower to develop relationships, they simply send out frigid e-mail memorandums. The best leaders, I think, are the ones who work hard at closing this gap. In my

own situation, one of the things we did was bringing in the

new recruits in the summer before their freshman year so they could get to know me better—so that when the season began, I was not intimidating to them.

Leadership, I believe, is *the key factor* in dealing with changing times. Leaders try to anticipate change and then adjust their own styles to suit it. Of course, there will always be unpredictability in the world. You can never anticipate everything that will happen. But *you can* take action yourself and *you can* create a culture that routinely adjusts to a changing environment.

That, I think, is one of the marks of great leadership. When poor leaders run their plans and encounter changing environments, they will often freeze up and say something like, "Well, I ran with the plan and it didn't work. I did everything I could."

But great leaders will anticipate the changes and spontaneously adjust to them. They'll encourage the members of their teams to take action on their own initiative. And they'll find new opportunities to score.

Effective leadership does not rest in the development of a plan alone. It results in the adjustment of that plan to meet the needs of a changing environment. As you grow in leadership, as you gain the confidence that comes from experience, you must allow yourself the opportunity to follow your instincts. You must make a play.

All of this also applies to our sport. Basketball is a beautiful team game. But teaching it to be played that way is now somewhat more problematic than it used to be. As college basketball's environment evolves, we have to evolve right along with it. An organization has to change to be good. And I'm not talking about just Duke being good, I'm talking about college basketball being good.

Leadership is not singular, it's plural. The NCAA should

305

team up with the NBA for the sake of our sport. Today in college basketball, we are unable to pinpoint any specific group that can make key decisions regarding the sport. Nobody is responsible! No one person is directly in charge! The NCAA treats every sport the same. There is no structure in place to make the decisions necessary to govern our game at the level it so richly deserves. It's no wonder then that we're dealing with rules and regulations that are no longer appropriate. It's time for changes! I have always been a proponent, for instance, of college basketball having a governing agency that is empowered to make key decisions on a day-to-day basis. It should fall under the NCAA umbrella and it should partner with the NBA to create new initiatives that will take basketball into the twenty-first century.

During the summer of 2004, I was presented with a choice of either staying in college basketball or going to the NBA. Perhaps the most storied franchise in professional basketball, the Los Angeles Lakers offered me an unbelievable amount of money to become their head coach. Actually, it came at an interesting time in my life. As I do at the end of every season, I was taking stock of who I was, where I was, and what I wanted to do in the future. In the past, I had quickly dismissed similar overtures. This time, though, I thought to myself, "Well, I'm fifty-seven years old, I've been at Duke twenty-four years—maybe I should listen to what the Lakers have to say."

Based upon my open and honest relationship with Duke, I spoke with Duke's president and athletic director before meeting face-to-face with the Lakers' management. Showing strength and self-confidence, Richard Brodhead and Joe Alleva encouraged me to investigate the opportunity. After securing their approval, I spoke personally with my coaches and staff. Then the Lakers came to town. I must say, I was astounded by the extent of their offer. It certainly made me stop and think twice. I mean, after all, such a package would not only provide financial security for my family, but also for my family's family. But the truth is that I've never made a decision based on what was going to make me the most money—and I didn't intend to start now.

In contemplating my decision, I relied heavily on my family for advice. My wife, Mickie, was especially helpful. She listened, asked questions, and helped me talk through all that I was feeling. At the beginning of the process, I asked myself if I still liked being a coach. Well, the answer was emphatic and passionate: "Yes. I still want to coach *and* teach for a long time to come." I also made up my mind that I wanted to continue to lead others. I realized that I very much enjoyed working with a group of people to achieve shared goals. *Because I believe in leading with the heart, I knew that I needed to follow my heart.* Then I started to relax—because I knew that I was going to both follow *and* lead with my heart. The question I then had to answer was where my heart really laid.

In my adult life, I feel fortunate to have been involved with the United States Military Academy, Duke University, and college basketball. Those three institutions are bigger than any individual or any group of individuals, and I have benefited greatly from being part of all three. For the past twenty-four years, Duke and college basketball have taken up my whole heart. I feel like I am really a part of this university in every aspect. And you really can't put a price tag on something like that. You just can't do it. Quite honestly, Duke has been the perfect place for me to coach, to teach, to lead, and to learn. I came to the realization that I really loved both Duke *and* college basketball. So the lure of this very prestigious position with the Los Angeles Lakers was weighed against that love. I decided to stay—*with* college basketball *at* Duke University.

At the end of the day, though, we all need to focus on something higher than basketball. For me, it's more about people, about life, about family. I'm frequently asked if the young people coming into our program are different today than they were, say, twenty years ago. Well, the kids are not different. They still want to play hard. They still want to be taught, to trust, to believe, and to love. Kids still want all these things. It's their culture that's changed, not them. It is their environment that's different.

As leaders, coaches, and as decent human beings, we owe it to our young people to help them develop their character as well as their jump shots. If we can provide them with a broad-based education, they will become more balanced, more knowledgeable, and more secure. And that helps everybody.

Over the years at Duke, we've tried to work with our players like a parent, a friend, or a brother. They are part of our family, in every way. And we have to be there for them when they need us. That's one reason we work so hard to maintain relationships with our players after they graduate and move on.

Why is that important? Well, for me personally, I believe that's one of the reasons we're here on earth. We must develop the gifts we are given. And just like none of us walks through life alone, none of us develops our gifts alone. It's a cooperative effort. We do it with the help of others—our parents, our friends, our teachers, our coaches. We do it as a team!

COACH K'S TIPS

- You can either change with your environment or you will eventually fail. A leader has to find a way to win.

- There is no failsafe way of doing things—no magic formula, no perfect recipe.

- In attempting new things and adjusting to change, you must not lower your standards. The basic values upon which you build your program do not change.

- Build relationships with the members of your team earlier and in more depth.

- Recruit people who have already demonstrated leadership skills.

- Remember that time is needed to develop deep relationships.

- Leadership relies very heavily on face-to-face communication.

- Leaders have to exert more direct control if their teams are inexperienced.

- Confidence is gained from experience.

- Reevaluate your situation regularly. Think in more depth and change accordingly. Then constantly adjust your methods to achieve better results.

- A leader doesn't have to be the only person doing the inspiring. Sometimes you can draw inspiration from the members of your own team.

- Experiment with your own leadership style and try to find out if there's a better way.

- Sometimes *who you think you are* and *who you are seen to be* are two different things.

- Work hard to close the gap between the stature you have attained and the hopes and dreams of the people in your organization.
- Leadership is *the key factor* in dealing with changing times.
- Create a culture that routinely adjusts to a changing environment.
- Follow your instincts. Make a play.

Note: A portion of the proceeds earned in adding this chapter to *Leading with the Heart* is being donated to the Emily Krzyzewski Family Life Center (www.emilykflc.com).

ACKNOWLEDGMENTS

We'd like to thank Larry Kirshbaum and Rick Wolff at Warner Books for their insight, encouragement, and support of this effort. We also appreciate all the hard work of Bob Barnett and Rob Urbach, our agents, in turning an idea into reality.

Gerry Brown, Johnny Dawkins, David Henderson, Grant Hill, Steve Wojciechowski, Quin Snyder, Tommy Amaker, and Jay Bilas all gave generously of their time and contributed significantly to key aspects of the manuscript. We thank them for their kindness and generosity.

A very special acknowledgment must go to Mickie Krzyzewski and Mike Cragg, who participated in virtually every step of the writing, editing, and creative process. Their long hours of dedication and commitment can never be fully realized by the readers, but we know and appreciate the important part they played in the creation of this book and we thank them for it.

Mike Krzyzewski
Don Phillips

INDEX

ABOUT THE AUTHORS

One of the leading ambassadors of college basketball, MIKE KRZYZEWSKI is Duke's all-time winningest coach. The 1999–2000 season marks his twentieth season at the helm of the Blue Devils' program.

Coach K became just the tenth coach in NCAA history to attain his five hundredth career victory, in his twenty-third season as a college head coach. The Chicago native began his coaching career at Army in 1975–1976 where he led the Cadets to an NIT appearance. He took over the Duke men's basketball program prior to the 1980–1981 season.

Coach K served as president of the National Association of Basketball Coaches (NABC) in 1998–1999 and is very much involved with several community groups, including the Duke Children's Hospital and nationally with the Jimmy V Foundation.

Entering the 1999–2000 season, Coach K was a six-time National Coach of the Year and five-time ACC Coach of the Year with a 48-13 all-time record in the NCAA tournament. Coach K has the most wins in the NCAA tournament among active coaches.

DONALD T. PHILLIPS is the author of six other books, including *Lincoln on Leadership, The Founding Fathers on Leadership,* and *Martin Luther King, Jr., on Leadership.* He currently serves as the mayor of Fairview, Texas.